BEATING BURNOUT

Mike McKinney is a registered clinical psychologist with over 30 years of experience. Following graduation from the University of Canterbury, Mike worked in mental health services before specializing in the management of persistent pain problems. More latterly, he has been working with increasing numbers of clients in his private practice who have been struggling with workplace stressors and burnout. Over the years, Mike has trained in several different martial arts, but his major recreation is the riding of his motorcycles. More recently, he has slipped down the rabbit hole of watch collecting. Mike lives in Christchurch, New Zealand, with his wife (also a psychologist). They have two young adult sons.

BEATING BURNOUT

HELPING THE ALL-OR-NOTHING PERSONALITY TO FIND BALANCE

MIKE McKINNEY

practical self-help tools by leading experts

First published 2025
Exisle Publishing Pty Ltd
PO Box 864, Chatswood, NSW 2057, Australia
226 High Street, Dunedin, 9016, New Zealand
www.exislepublishing.com

Copyright © 2025 in text: Mike McKinney

Mike McKinney asserts the moral right to be identified as the author of this work.

All rights reserved. Except for short extracts for the purpose of review, no part of this book may be reproduced, stored in a retrieval system or transmitted in any form or by any means, whether electronic, mechanical, photocopying, recording or otherwise, without prior written permission from the publisher.

A CiP record for this book is available from the National Library of Australia.

ISBN 978-1-923011-06-9

Designed by Shaun Jury
Typeset in Miller Text Roman 9.5/14pt
Printed in China

This book uses paper sourced under ISO 14001 guidelines from well-managed forests and other controlled sources.

10 9 8 7 6 5 4 3 2 1

Note
This book is inspired by and based on, an earlier title by the author, *All or Nothing: Bringing balance to the achievement-oriented personality*. While the principles discussed remain the same, the content has been adapted to provide a sharper focus on the topic of burnout and its management. The quote by Employment Today on the front cover is taken from a review of this earlier work.

Disclaimer
This book is a general guide only and should never be a substitute for the skill, knowledge and experience of a qualified medical professional dealing with the facts, circumstances and symptoms of a particular case. The information presented in this book is based on the research, training and professional experience of the author, and is true and complete to the best of their knowledge. However, this book is intended only as an informative guide; it is not intended to replace or countermand the advice given by the reader's personal physician. Because each person and situation is unique, the author and the publisher urge the reader to check with a qualified healthcare professional before using any procedure where there is a question as to its appropriateness. The author, publisher and their distributors are not responsible for any adverse effects or consequences resulting from the use of the information in this book. It is the responsibility of the reader to consult a physician or other qualified healthcare professional regarding their personal care. The intent of the information provided is to be helpful; however, there is no guarantee of results associated with the information provided.

*'When the student is ready, the teacher will appear.'
My journey towards becoming a clinician has not just involved textbooks, lectures and conferences. I have gained much from the people in my life. So, many thanks to my family and friends from across the years. Without realizing it, you have imparted wisdom, knowledge and skills to me, by being yourselves and simply doing you.*

CONTENTS

1. Making sense of burnout — *1*
2. Who is more likely to develop burnout? — *10*
3. Where (and why) did this approach begin? — *30*
4. What keeps this all going? — *44*
5. Turning the tide — *63*
6. The harsh internal critic: an unhelpful passenger — *82*
7. Striving for perfection, or needing to be perfect? — *101*
8. Health and wellbeing — *120*
9. New perspectives, achievement, and the 'me' — *146*
10. Plotting a (future) life course amidst and beyond burnout — *174*
11. Building for the future, despite the uncertainty of burnout — *187*
12. The partner's journey (or the canary in the coalmine) — *200*
    Conclusion — *213*
    Bibliography — *218*
    Index — *220*

1.
MAKING SENSE OF BURNOUT

In the modern working world, burnout is often seen as a disease. However, the concept, and indeed identification, of burnout is not all that new. Companies have been aware of burnout for decades and the industrial/organizational arms of psychology have studied and written much about it.

In essence, burnout is a personal response to regularly engaging in high-demand situations over extended periods. It is a multidimensional concept but one that tends to have some key components, which we will explore together throughout this book. We will also be looking closely at what you can do to bring about positive change — whether you are developing burnout or are already living the experience.

At the core of burnout is a sense of emotional tiredness or even exhaustion. This comes about due to the ongoing nature of the job demands and the realities of trying to function in your life. This is particularly so when you are consistently operating at a level that requires more from you than you are receiving or replenishing. Alongside this is a type of intellectual or cognitive tiredness that presents itself as a loss of sharpness and reduced ability to do previously normal cognitive tasks. People also tend to experience reduced physical and personal energy, often in contrast to what they previously had.

Perhaps one of the most problematic aspects of burnout is the creeping sense of dissatisfaction, which can lead to cynicism. The latter can be about your role, the company worked for or even about yourself (i.e. who you are, what you have achieved and where you are heading). It's a bit like an existential train wreck, something that calls into question the very foundation of who you are and how you have been operating.

But burnout is not inevitable. It does not affect everyone with a demanding job or busy life. Nor is it going to last forever. Part of the secret to helping prevent burnout seems to relate to your motivation for undertaking the task or role you are in — for example, if you are motivated to stay in a high-pressure position by your own reasons and values, rather than by external factors or payoffs, this is protective. If you are working towards goals and outcomes that are relevant and consistent with your values (more on these later), there is less chance you will become overwhelmed and then burnt out. This is because the goals are consistent with who you are and what is important to you (i.e. not related purely to reinforcers such as increased money or respect from others). There is also an association between intrinsically identified goals and enhanced feelings of personal wellbeing, a positive sense of self and confidence in doing things.

WHO EXPERIENCES BURNOUT?

Burnout is a phenomenon that comes about as a result of experiencing ongoing (usually high) levels of pressure and stress. It is important to acknowledge that the effects can be experienced by people operating in a number of roles, such as medical students or people in long-term, non-paid caring roles. However, the World Health Organization defines burnout as 'resulting from chronic workplace stress that has not been successfully managed' and relates to it within the occupational context. For this reason, and due to my professional experience of increasing numbers of professional clients presenting with the symptoms of burnout, this book focuses on the workplace and discusses this as the main cause of burnout. However, if you are experiencing burnout-related symptoms due to other roles or reasons, the book and techniques discussed will still be very helpful for you.

While the research identifies that the most effective way to address burnout is through changes in the workplace, it is unlikely that you — a person currently experiencing burnout — are in a position to effect these changes. So this book focuses instead on what you can do: it will show you ways to help regain a sense of control by looking at aspects of yourself that could make you more vulnerable to burnout in the first place.

WHY DO WE NEED TO KNOW ABOUT BURNOUT?

It's important to understand burnout as it affects you as an individual, as a worker/professional, as a partner and family member, as a parent, as a friend — in every role you have in life. Burnout affects you at an emotional level as well as a behavioural one. It can impact your mental focus and energy and it comes from ... your workplace.

Burnout is not a contagion that you catch in the main street of town, nor is it transmitted through contact/poor hygiene. It emanates from the environment you are in, such as the workplace, and the factors that operate within that setting. These can include the stressors and demands of the role itself or the unrelenting workload you are exposed to over long periods of time and that seem impossible to deal with. It is also a stealthy condition that quietly takes hold of your life and then manages to suck out the enjoyment, focus and energy from deep within you. It doesn't hit you all of a sudden. Rather, it operates like the slow leak of your car tyre, where the air (or your energy) quietly but consistently leaks out until it reaches a point where the tyre no longer operates as it did previously. Try driving your car with one or two tyres like that and see what it does to the performance and capabilities of a previously well-running machine. If you keep driving like that, there will be a noticeable difference in the time it takes to get to places compared to previous journeys, and you run the risk of doing permanent damage to important parts of your vehicle. Now, transpose the tyre for yourself and the escaping air for your depleting energy. Get the picture?

Burnout does not occur within a vacuum. It is associated with the stressors and demands of your workplace and comes about from the expectation to perform to a high level, over a long period of time and, often, without adequate resources. It is the combination of these factors which really determines burnout's overall effect on you. Any one of these issues may be a challenge by itself; however, when several of these key ingredients appear together and remain present for a long period of time, the effects are almost exponential. This is especially so when you have no recovery time or space, as the expectations and productivity demands remain the same. As a result, you tend to keep trying to perform as expected (or as you expect of yourself!) and the toll begins to mount.

Throughout the book I'll introduce you to some techniques and ideas to help you calm your nervous system and reframe the way you relate to burnout and your approach to work, starting with a breathing technique, below.

TRY THIS

Simple breathing exercises are a portable, go-anywhere way to help you manage stress and nervous system arousal, both of which are present during burnout. Deep, diaphragmatic breathing (sometimes called 'belly breathing') helps to slow the heart rate, regulate blood pressure and reduce levels of cortisol — the stress hormone — in the blood.

To start, try the technique below or do a quick internet search for other styles that might suit you.

Box breathing

Begin by sitting in a chair that has a back, or gently lean against a wall. This is for physical support and sensory feedback that you are safe. Close your eyes and shift your attention to your breathing. Breathe out slowly, letting all the air leave your lungs. Now:

- Breathe in through your nose while counting to four in your head. (Make the in-breath slow and steady, and try to notice the sensation of air filling your lungs.)
- Hold the breath in your lungs as you count to four.
- Slowly and steadily (don't rush it) exhale through your mouth, as you count to four.
- Pause (briefly, not breathing) for a count of four.

Making sense of burnout

> Start the cycle again by breathing for four, and repeat the cycle until you feel calmer or more settled.

The effects of burnout do not remain exclusively in the workplace; you will experience the associated difficulties in all facets of your life. If you think about it, it's pretty hard to conceive of a way that significant stress and its associated negative personal changes would remain within the four walls of your workplace. These experiences are going to be carried home with you and expressed in all domains of your life. Interestingly, and unfortunately, you most likely did not notice this burnout beginning to impact your work performance. As a result, there is a high chance you will not notice that it is affecting how you relate to your world, the people around you and the things that you previously found to be positive or interesting.

WHAT CAUSES BURNOUT?

Let's start by getting one thing out of the way. People don't become burnt out simply because they are unhappy in their job. That might make you feel stressed or dissatisfied, but it is not the same as burnout. You might not enjoy your role at work and may not want to be part of the organization, but this is not the same as the fatigue, emotional distancing and cynicism that characterizes burnout.

If we are to understand burnout better, we need to start where it starts: the workplace. This book isn't going to focus specifically on your work situation or what you can do within that to feel better. But we do need to first understand the central role that work can play in burnout showing up in your life. As you probably know, one of the biggest drivers in developing burnout is being overworked. This involves too much to do and, often, too little time to do it in. This can also be compounded by not having enough resources available to do your work. Not having the right tools, or having timeframes that are too tight, can result in you staying later at work (possibly without compensation), missing your breaks or feeling like you cannot take leave. The result of this is that there is no time to switch off from work or disengage cognitively from the demands of the role. This is particularly so if you have a work phone, which can receive messages at all hours of the day or night. As a result, your role does not necessarily finish when you leave the office — nor does the concern and worry around completing tasks!

More generally, expectations and workplace practices can also have a big effect on the development of burnout. Often referred to as the culture of the company, this relates to both explicit (as well as implicit) expectations. There can be verbal statements/directions as well as modelled behaviours; for example, if those in charge never seem to take breaks or often leave late. If they work through their lunch breaks and stay beyond the usual finishing time, this can send messages to the team that this is how things are done.

A confusing and subtle shaper of office behaviours can come in the form of mixed messages. The most challenging of these is when a company has publicly stated guidelines for healthy-working behaviours — such as advice to care for yourself, statements on the importance of taking time for yourself and not going beyond what is realistic — yet the upper echelons of the team demonstrate different behaviours. How do you look after yourself when the bosses are seen to work very long hours on a consistent basis and your regular meetings are focused on achieving unrealistic targets?

The issue of team culture can play a large role in demonstrating what is considered 'correct' within a workplace and can have a significant impact on the company's employees. The unspoken language can be one of preferring hard work within an environment with 'values' around ensuring targets are achieved. This preference may be expressed via interactions (who the bosses spend more time with) or reinforcements (e.g. increased salaries and consideration for advancement). These potential outcomes are monitored by employees and it is often very hard to resist the unspoken — but clearly obvious — preferences of the seniors. As a result, the expectations get picked up, taken on board and then reinforced, which of course means this approach to work is maintained. Such an approach can be particularly challenging if you do not feel confident within yourself at work, or if you operate with an 'all or nothing' approach (we'll explore this soon). This can lead you to either operate within the preferred, achieving manner or else run the risk of becoming an employee who is not valued.

A disconnect between the organization's and an employee's value sets can have a significant impact on burnout. The greater the gap, the more often staff find themselves making a trade-off between how they are expected to operate and how they would prefer to operate.

When we feel as if we are not making any headway (despite high levels of effort or many hours at work), then we are more likely to experience burnout. This is because, despite our valiant efforts to meet goals and aims, we develop and then grow the notion that nothing is making any difference. It's a bit like trying to wade through a swampy patch of land that grabs your boots and sucks them in further with each step you take. The effort required to keep going forward starts to take its toll after a while, but you realize that you can't really stop in the middle of a swampy patch of ground. This seems to leave you with little choice other than to keep pushing on, while worrying that you might not make it to the other side. Try to hold that image in your head for a few moments and think about what the loss of energy and heightened struggle might do to you, your confidence and all aspects of your life outside of work. Perhaps you can see from this image what happens when you become tired and overwhelmed while feeling trapped in a particular workplace or role.

2.
WHO IS MORE LIKELY TO DEVELOP BURNOUT?

There are two aspects to consider when looking into this question. One is whether certain occupational groups might be more susceptible to burnout. The second is which personal characteristics could make it more likely that you develop the condition. In this chapter we will explore both of these important issues, as they can have interactive and synergistic effects. As you read on, you might find you work in one of the occupational groups known to have high levels of burnout. This is not all bad news, as such awareness can give you a chance to catch things before they become too bad. Similarly, by developing an understanding of personal attributes or characteristics that could make it more likely you'll develop burnout, you can reflect upon how you behave and operate within the workplace. This, again, should give you the opportunity to see whether your relationship to work may be setting you up for a not-so-good outcome. Some readers might tick boxes in both camps — this is a double whammy, but forewarned is forearmed!

Having said that, it is vital to reiterate a most important point: anyone, in any working role or industry, can develop burnout. However, some industries do seem more likely to set their employees up to experience high levels of stress and burnout. As noted earlier, this may be because of limited resources or due to expectations. Just because a person chooses to work in a certain industry does not mean they are fully aware of the real-life implications of operating in that domain. Within these occupational groups, there will be a significant contribution from the way the business operates. Conditions that are set up to maximize output and the generation of billable hours will probably have a greater effect on workers' wellbeing. This is due to the prioritization process, which would focus on achieving aims and goals, rather than looking after employees. The organizational aspects of the workplace will affect the workers' quality of work experience — and potentially their longevity in the industry.

As children, all of us encountered modelling of behaviours in our family of origin, school and social settings — we would have viewed the activities and behaviours of important people in our lives. As a result, we will have probably repeated those behaviours and put in place others that are similar, as we unconsciously absorbed the messaging that such behaviours were desirable. Something very similar occurs in the workplace and, although adults, we are just as vulnerable to these paradigms. If your supervisor or colleagues all demonstrate similar ways of working, you will quickly figure out that to get ahead you have to behave in a similar manner. Reinforcement contingencies are still relevant for us as grown-up people. You and I both respond to praise by continuing the praised behaviour. As we are social and herd creatures, we generally want to do as the tribe does, so that we can fit in and be considered worthy tribe members. And guess what? Once we have been behaving for a while in the ways valued by the tribe, we internalize them as being part of the tribe culture and automatically continue exhibiting them.

Burnout doesn't just happen to one 'type' of person. However, there can be some similarities amongst the people who experience burnout, not the least of which is pushing yourself to attain goals while being concerned about judgments from others and only feeling good when you meet targets you set. If you are struggling at work and find your sense of self is precariously balanced or dependant on feedback from external people and organizations, you may well be at risk of experiencing burnout.

It is not all bad news, though. People less likely to experience burnout are those who identify positively with their role. This is important, because if you can begin to shift your emphasis from achieving for achievement's sake, you will reduce your risk of developing burnout. A key message here is that there are risks to focusing on the outcomes alone (particularly in the longer term).

Hopefully, you will see from this chapter that how you operate can have implications for your health — both physical and psychological.

THE JOB MADE ME DO IT

Some businesses and professions operate in ways that present a bigger risk of developing burnout. Regardless of your profession, if you are pushed beyond your ability to cope for long enough, you are more likely to suffer burnout. If you work in one of the professions explored below, it's even more important to take note of both the causes and solutions to burnout — especially if you are in a leadership role.

The legal profession

Although many professions have highly committed people working in them, there are some that attract (or is that create?) a higher proportion of such people. One of these is the legal profession. This is a group of very focused individuals in a profession that values tradition, doing things correctly and working very hard. There is a high risk for burnout in the legal profession because of consistently high workloads, tight deadlines and a seeming dedication to long hours in order to rise through the ranks. It is also peopled by individuals who are intelligent, competitive and driven to achieve. I recall phone calls with a friend when he was practising law in the United States. He would describe how he had finally finished his work around 2 a.m. but that there was little point in heading home because he would no sooner be settled into sleep than he'd need to get up to start the next workday. As he progressed and honed his talents, he became more used to doing the long hours and described negotiations that would go till the early hours, which then necessitated him returning to his office to type up contracts to be presented at the start of the next business day. He also described the expectation for new employees: that they would fully commit themselves to the company and its aims. Interestingly, this expectation was not necessarily articulated but, I would suggest, it soon became apparent to new employees by watching the behaviours of the partners and other senior lawyers. When I asked what would happen to a new person who did not undertake long hours, I was told that nothing would actively happen to them; however, they would probably not advance within the company. Now what are the chances that this unarticulated, informal message would go unnoticed?

Psychological research provides some insight into the legal profession and those who pursue it. It appears that, as a group, lawyers are impacted by psychological distress to a greater level than both the general population and other occupational groups. It is hypothesized that personality traits prevalent amongst lawyers may make them more vulnerable to depression and anxiety. The personality traits this group regularly exhibit include a very strong work ethic, competitiveness, perfectionism, and a need for achievement. The question of interest for us is whether such commitment comes at a cost for the individual and whether the profession attracts and/or actively selects those who may exhibit this focused and very disciplined approach to work. This type of commitment to the role can result in an imbalance between home, personal and work life. Such an imbalance is regularly identified as one of the predictors of burnout.

The caring professions: doctors, nurses, social workers, counsellors, psychologists

Why might it be that people who are caring — and even promote self-care — are prone to experience burnout? It seems to make little intuitive sense when mental and physical health professionals spend their time helping others to cope better and manage challenges more effectively. Seems more than a little ironic, doesn't it? However, one of the core attributes of people in the caring professions is that they care about people and their wellbeing. This can lead to an intense focus on helping others but not necessarily themselves. Their training and social conscience leads people in these professions to prioritize the needs of their clients/patients. Perhaps being a caring individual should come with a healthcare announcement: 'Warning! Being extremely caring to others may be injurious to your own wellbeing.' Sounds silly when you say it like that, I guess. However, when you have a client base with consistently high needs and their situations really speak to your own emotions, you are less likely to place boundaries on your time.

No matter where you are in the world, the health professions are underfunded and under-resourced. These two factors can lead to clinicians putting in longer hours, plugging gaps in the system/rosters and going beyond their physical tolerance levels. Unfortunately, once the clinical work is done for the day, there tends to be a pile of admin work still to do, which extends work hours. When you care greatly about others, you tend to downplay or overlook your own needs, as these seem to pale in comparison. This is why exhaustion — a key component of burnout — is prevalent in such workers. Whether you are working in the emergency department of your local hospital or providing support in a mental health setting, there are many interpersonal demands that require you to not only be present but also empathetic with each client/patient you encounter, across each day. There are also upsetting aspects to such jobs. The stories clinicians hear and the significant health problems encountered have the potential to wear anyone down over time.

Caring and helping are not attributes limited to paid professionals, of course. There are millions of people worldwide who are caring for family members with chronic health problems or intellectual, physical or psychiatric disabilities. This can involve long hours of providing physical and emotional support and tends to see the carer placing their family member's needs front and centre. What drives these carers is not monetary gain but caring, and the desire to have their loved one looked after in the best possible way. As the role is often within the family home, it can mean that the one doing the caring, quite literally, cannot get away from the tasks at hand. Over time, this high level of activity and being fully emotionally present can take its toll.

Dan is a wonderfully caring man in his fifties. He lives with his husband, who has significant and disabling health issues. The couple has been happily married for years and the love remains strong. However, Dan came to my office seeking help for his feelings of absolute tiredness, a distancing from the partner he cared for and loved, plus a sense that nothing was ever going to change. He disliked the fact he was struggling — because this was his husband and how could anyone become sad and pessimistic in a loving environment?

Although Dan had funded carer hours available, it appeared that he was often doing many of the tasks that the assistants were employed to do. When I explored this more closely, Dan began describing a fear that his husband might not get the high level of care he needed, or that the other carers might not really understand what his husband needed. Dan was also acutely aware of the multitude of risks to his husband's vulnerable health. So, to ensure he did not go without and to minimize risks to him, Dan would often do (or redo) tasks the carers undertook. For surely no one could care for his husband as well and lovingly as he could. This approach was driven by a mixture of perfectionism, strong schemas around responsibility and fear for his husband's wellbeing. The result was the experience of burnout.

Business professions

One of the groups I really enjoy working with are executives and managers from the business world. They tend to be bright, goal-oriented and keen to achieve. They are also notoriously bad at noticing when things have started to get out of balance in their lives and work environments.

Ironically, while business professionals often have oversight of large budgets and sensitive timelines, which require attention to detail, and are often in charge of departments and team members, it seems to elude them that they may not actually be in control of their own missions and behaviours. However, it may not always be about not noticing personal changes. There can be some strong pressures within the upper echelons of business to always be on top of things and demonstrate leadership by being all things to all people. This can come with a hefty price tag for some people, as they feel a pressure to not show 'weakness' within the corporate world. Additionally, there may be few confidantes at the higher levels of business who are not direct competitors. The old adage of it being lonely at the top may well be true. Where do you go to seek support if the expectation is that you should be running everything and 'onto it'?

One of the fears that traps senior executives into soldiering on is that their reputation could suffer and the demanding corporate world might not want to hire someone who has had 'difficulties'. (This, of course, underscores why burnout is insidious and so hard to reduce in the workforce.) If people do not want to acknowledge they are experiencing it, how can it ever be normalized and 'okay' for individuals to experience? We know that unrelenting pressure contributes to burnout, and the pressures at the top of the company can be particularly onerous due to their multidimensional nature and competing demands.

These include meeting the expectations of disparate groups such as the workforce, board and shareholders.

In the business world, I have come across a small group of leaders I have found hard to work with on the issue of burnout. These are entrepreneurs and founders of start-up companies — particularly within the tech industries. By the time they make contact with me they have often been working full-time in their fledgling company for a couple of years. This has invariably involved very long hours, a high sense of responsibility, a lot of investment (time, money and emotional connection) plus a powerful level of passion. Unfortunately, by the time of our meeting, they have all (to a person) been experiencing unpleasant feelings for quite some time. Their moods are variable to low, they report poor sleep, reduced energy and — for the first time — a sense that they are less connected somehow to the direction of their business 'babies'. This is wrapped up in a cocoon of struggle around the venture, which involves doubts creeping in about anything from its worthiness to the utility of their product.

The above feelings and experiences are often alien to this group of young and, usually, energetic individuals. It makes no sense to them why they don't feel energized each morning to tackle the latest issue or funding application. To use a psychological term, this is ego-dystonic ... and they hate feeling like this. The aim of engaging in therapy is clear to these successful and focused young people. They want answers and tools to fix these uncomfortable sensations and feelings. Interestingly, most of them also read extensively on burnout and a number will have already signed up for yoga, meditation or mindfulness courses (or apps). Time proves to be critical for these clients, as they are used to addressing problems, identifying solutions and moving on. They also prefer strategies that they can 'do' to settle the discomfort and get them back on track. The real challenges with such clients come when I suggest that two central aspects of managing burnout are making changes to a demanding workplace environment and being open to adjusting behaviours, plus expectations in relation to performance and achievement. The first point proves to be unacceptable, as their passion tells them this was how it needs to be. The second point is unacceptable, as their passion once again tells them this was how it needs to be.

PERSONAL FACTORS THAT CONTRIBUTE TO BURNOUT

Are there similarities in each of the professional groups outlined above, I hear you ask? I believe the answer is yes. There are personal attributes that underpin the choice of individuals to enter these professions and then regularly go above and beyond the call of duty. These are known as *schemas* and we will explore these as we progress through the book. For now, remember this word and be curious about it, as later on I will ask you to consider which types of schemas you operate by.

Each of us is an individual and we bring aspects of our own self to the workplace and how we engage in tasks/roles. These can be strengths that help us to navigate our way through the demands of a role, or they can be attributes that become vulnerabilities in certain settings. In identifying these characteristics, there is no suggestion that a person is to blame for developing burnout. Rather, by understanding these attributes you can enhance your understanding of the issues that might contribute to the experience. By knowing these aspects, you can develop new ways to take care of yourself, make changes so you can move away from burnout, or prevent it from becoming an issue in the first place. I would like to put forward that having this understanding opens an avenue for you to reclaim your sense of control in a world that has become upsetting, possibly chaotic and is affecting your life to a large extent. This is because the contributing factors that are 'within you' are things you can work on and alter. The benefit is that you become a director of change in your life and an architect of your recovery.

Alongside the schemas, we will explore other internal/personal attributes and consider how you can manage their influence upon you, your decisions and behaviours. These will include:

- The way you make sense of your role and its demands. This can include how fairly you feel you are being treated and how equitably you perceive the workload is being distributed.
- There is another side to this appraisal process that is relevant to the concept of burnout. This is where you make sense of everything as being important and feel you need to perform to ever increasing levels. If everything is seen as urgent, the only (perceived) choice is to push on, despite dwindling personal resources, and try to meet what you believe is required.

TRY THIS

If you view everything as urgent, you will soon get overwhelmed. However, if everything is urgent, then nothing is actually urgent — because everything is the same. One management strategy is to use the skill of prioritization, which will let you see which tasks need to be addressed first, so you can bring some order to the chaos and tick things off of the list. However, my experience is that this doesn't work so well if you are under the pump and feel you cannot order anything. To shift from this place of overwhelm and helplessness, I encourage my clients to adopt a triage model, to break through this impasse of *everything* being perceived as critical.

The triage model of medicine was developed during wartime, when medical teams had limited resources and personnel to help the at times overwhelming numbers of injured soldiers. The approach acknowledges that every injured soldier is valued and their life is important. However, instead of judging one as being more deserving, the model's guidelines addressed the grim reality of the situation. Soldier A might be in agony but is not about to die; Soldier B is in agony and has an injury that definitely needs a procedure/surgery but they would still be alive in, say, four hours; in terrible pain yes, but still alive. On the other hand, Soldier C has an injury requiring immediate attention or else they will simply not survive. In this scenario, Soldier C is considered the top priority because of the extent of their need and the risks of non-responding.

The basis of the triage model is to help make a choice in a situation that feels like there is no way to differentiate between patients. It brings things down to the most critical issues and highlights the cost of inaction, so a clearer order can be established. I want to suggest that this is also possible within the workplace.

> Next time you are faced with multiple 'priorities', ask yourself: what will be the negative consequences/outcomes if this issue is not immediately addressed? Acknowledge that all priorities are relevant, but rank them according to your answer to the above question for each task.

Here are a few more important points to remember about personal attributes and how they affect your propensity towards burnout:

- If you do not feel you can make any sort of change, you are more likely to start feeling helpless and then lose your sense of control. Burnout is then just a step around the corner.
- Some people, regardless of their job, have a strong feeling that they need to be in control of all aspects of the operation or task. The result can be to simply push harder to establish that elusive sense of control.
- Struggling with uncertainty: if your role at work is ill defined, you don't know what is required of you and there is limited feedback on your performance, the result is a stressful situation that can wear you down. A common response to this situation is to deliver at a very high level, assuming you then must surely have met the target and achieved what your manger requires of you. Psychological research shows us that uncertainty can be a powerful stressor with both psychological and physiological consequences.
- Top performers and perfectionists are essentially two sides of the same coin. What they have in common is an

internal drive to achieve, often to a standard that is self-set. People who operate like this tend to take on more than their fair share. They also continue working at tasks until they feel the task is completed 'satisfactorily' (decode this as 'to the highest possible standard').

Finally, being good at your job is risky. In my practice, I provide clinical input to members of the armed forces. Within the forces there is a term known as 'performance punishment'. This identifies that individuals who excel at their roles tend to be given more work and a broadening of the scope of their roles. The thinking behind this appears to be that an important task is best given to those who have shown their capabilities. In effect, they are 'punished' for doing so well by being given extra duties and roles. A problem with this (and one that fits with the descriptor of punishment) is that their current workload is never really taken into account or reduced. The assumption is that such high performers can handle whatever is thrown at them. An unhelpful aspect of the impacted individual's personality is that they tend not to say no. Unfortunately, such achievers tend not to notice (or even consider) the impact of this on themselves.

TRY THIS

Attempting to place boundaries in your workplace can feel threatening. It brings up images of being judged as not good enough or not working hard enough. Neither of these feels good. However, being able to place some limits on what is given to you can be the first step in getting some balance back in your life.

Being assertive is a good thing, but needs to be done appropriately and it takes time to feel confident doing it. Just saying 'no' when stressed may be a little too reactive and can sound aggressive. A middle ground is to find a way to convey that you would like to help but are busy and cannot fit everything in. Try saying something along the lines of: 'If I understand you right, you would like me to do X and have it ready by the end of the week. Given the other projects I am currently working on for you, which would you prefer that I put on hold to be able to fit in this task?'

This does two things. First, it lets the other party know that you are currently very busy. Second, it puts the onus onto the requester to make a call on the priorities.

If you are a 'yes' person, try doing what managers always do when you ask for a pay rise. They take the heat out of the moment by deferring a decision until they have had time to consider everything and then they will 'get back to you'. When you are asked to help out (and you feel a strong sense of obligation), try saying, 'I would like to assist with that if possible; I'll check my diary and get back to you once I know what I already have scheduled.' This is not agreeing and then instantly regretting it. It is not feeling scared you will offend the other person. It is also not responding in an automatic manner. The result is that you get breathing space to consider what this request might add to your current workload and then you can decide whether to take it on.

ALL-OR-NOTHING (A/N) PERSONALITY STYLE

An 'all-or-nothing' person has many positive attributes, not the least of which is the ability to focus on a task and see it through to completion. Such people are often praised for their achievements and are self-reinforced for their efforts. People with an A/N personality tend to prioritize the immediate, positive outcomes such as completion, which then becomes both a motivator and a reinforcer. To this end, the person is willing to trade off other, potentially competing demands and activities in order to meet the self-generated goal. Being busy is a central theme of an A/N person's life and this busyness is always in service of a particular goal (e.g. short-term projects or longer-term career strategies). Although they might be given tasks by their employer or manager, an important element is their internal drive. This involves an ability to filter out distractions and 'unnecessary' events, allowing complete focus and setting the scene for undisturbed application of effort.

To the A/N individual, there appears to be but one way to move forward and that invariably involves pushing oneself. While this is useful for achieving and completing, it can come at a cost. The individual can overlook consequences that are not necessarily obvious but may be building up. Such costs can be health related, socially oriented, employment based, familial or recreational. This totality of focus often means these 'other' issues or tasks are downgraded in importance — not purposely, it must be said, but because they don't fit the current brief and therefore are simply not registered. Over time, this approach can become a self-perpetuating system that limits and narrows awareness, which further reduces the potential for flexibility. Thus, the concept of balance in life can be lost, or at least not considered.

Time away from the current work-related activities is seen as a problem and life can eventually hit a tipping point whereby other interests, obligations and relationships start to take a back seat.

Once an A/N person is fully engaged in a task, strong aspects of their personality (such as a sense of responsibility and commitment) start to kick in and this makes it increasingly hard for them to shift from their main focus. Part of why this is difficult is that task completion can be intimately intertwined with the need to do a perfect job. Ceasing a task partway through seems to equate with a sense of failure, and this fear of failure can be the driver of much of the behaviour that has become 'all or nothing'. If you operate like this at work, there is going to be a selecting of attention and a prioritization process that places work needs to the fore. This can result in you driving yourself to achieve within the single forum of work, not having any balance in wider life, and moving towards a situation where you may experience burnout.

The combination of high expectations and motivation is a powerful one and can mean the A/N person persists with tasks when others might have called a halt. This can be positive with regard to deadlines or the meeting of a performance goal. However, it can be unhelpful when self-monitoring is suspended in deference to the bigger goal. The only variables accounted for at such times are those directly related to the outcome of the project at hand. Perhaps not such an issue if the project is measured in hours or days, but potentially problematic if it relates to an ongoing role or longer-term goal, such as a career pathway.

'All or nothing' is an approach to and way of engaging with life. It is an expression of personal characteristics. It is also something that has helped you achieve, potentially to high levels. Unfortunately, it can set you up to tune out from the changes in your wellbeing — as they may conflict with the demands of the role. Fatigue (both physical and cognitive) is often experienced by such individuals, but their goal orientation will mean they downplay or explain away why they are feeling so tired on a regular basis. Additionally, the primacy of work requirements will leave little time for opportunities to engage in interesting or relaxing events. Taken together, these issues can bring about that psychological and personal distancing from the work role and environment that is characteristic of burnout. Within the workplace, this personality style can be an advantage (up to a point), but the narrowing of focus will become a vulnerability.

PULLING ALL THIS TOGETHER

Any, or all, of the above can contribute to burnout. However, the more of these factors that are operating, the higher the chance that burnout will occur. These factors interact with each other, feed off each other and can become overwhelming.

There is no doubt that experiencing burnout will impact you and your sense of wellbeing, but it will also affect your relationships with people close to you. To understand the far-reaching nature of burnout, visualize for a moment what happens when you drop a pebble into a pond of water. The pebble impacts one spot (the burnout symptoms affecting you) but the effects of that impact radiate outwards across the pond. These ripples that you see moving outwards (the effects from the burnout) touch whatever is in the near vicinity (think close family). As these ripples move further from the point of impact (you), they lose some of their power but the effects are still noticeable (your friends and co-workers). Eventually, the ripples will settle and have no impact on the far reaches of the pond (your community) but they will have altered anything they encountered, even for a brief moment.

The risk with burnout is that it has the potential to affect us — physically, emotionally, cognitively and behaviourally. These effects will be experienced in all aspects of our lives, including how we interact with people we know and care about.

REFLECTION EXERCISES

Exercise 1

Make a list of as many things as you can that motivate you or act as payoffs/reinforcers in your employment. Now go down this list and beside each one write an 'I' if it is an Internal motivator or reinforcer, or an 'E' if it is an external one. Count them up and see which predominates. What does this show you and what might it suggest about your approach to work-related activities?

Now, consider how these behaviours sit with who you are and what is important to you. Is there a close fit between the way you have been behaving at work and what is truly important to you? Or have things become unbalanced? If the exercise suggests you are motivated by external factors and payoffs, it is possible that this is driving you in a direction and/or to an extent that is starting to clash with what is meaningful to you. If you bring to mind what you have just read, burnout is more likely if you are driving yourself for external reasons and to attain outcomes that are not necessarily central to the real you.

Exercise 2

Following on from the above exercise, ask yourself: What do I need to help me **engage** with work, rather than be enslaved by it? It might be time to check in with your attitude and understanding around your work role and efforts. Is there a gap (or perhaps even a chasm!) between how you initially envisioned yourself behaving and what you have actually been doing?

If you are approaching and then engaging with your role in a way that fits closely with your true interests and desires, there is a greater likelihood you will have a fulfilling relationship with the role. As a result, it may also be more enjoyable and sustainable for you. However, if your role has been dominating your life to the point where other previously enjoyed activities have disappeared, something is not gelling.

3.
WHERE (AND WHY) DID THIS APPROACH BEGIN?

Most people who push themselves have been behaving the same way for a long time — the executive who works all hours did not just suddenly become like that. But these behaviours, often exhibited across a range of areas (or domains) of life, can become more obvious (and also potentially problematic) once the person finds their niche in life. No matter which environment the behaviour is expressed in, people who operate like this share key attributes. Prime amongst these is an orientation towards perfection, a drive to succeed and a readiness to push themselves to meet their goal/s. The question is whether these attributes were made, developed or stumbled upon.

WHERE WE COME FROM CAN BE IMPORTANT

If you ask people with burnout about their earliest recollections of behaviours such as pushing themselves, they often state that their family of origin had a set of values which revolved around meeting goals and/or having high standards. Allied with this may have been expectations around performance and involvement in tasks — for example, homework and chores being completed, and to a high standard. The person's parents might have been people who worked hard, prioritized completion and valued good outcomes. Thus, there was potentially a good degree of modelling involved. This would have been observed, if not yet fully understood, by the child. By watching a credible role model — someone important, trusted, respected (or feared) — engage in tasks and repeatedly respond in a particular way, the child starts to accept that this is how things are done.

Within the family, contingencies will operate that reinforce certain behaviours and approaches, such as completing a task *before* moving on to more enjoyable activities. These expectations might be referred to regularly, so that they become part of how the family operates. Positive reinforcement might also flow more readily when the child meets the expectations so they learn that working hard, fast and to a good standard are valued by significant others. Additionally, these ways of behaving lead to social reinforcement, positive standing and possibly rewards (e.g. treats or pocket money). Conversely, not performing to a certain level or in a manner consistent with expectations might lead to a cost, such as punishment or loss of access to rewards. Such learning is powerful. If the standards are set and reinforced by significant people, a strong desire to please others (by meeting these expectations) can develop.

Over time, such expectations can become part of the family ethos, culture and experience. The norms are set and they determine behavioural approaches for those in the family system. The young person will then take these beliefs and expectations of behaviour with them as they move outside the family environment and into other circles, such as school or sporting arenas. Even at a relatively early age, children can demonstrate a focus on task completion and quality of engagement. If this is connected with positive outcomes (e.g. a sense of success or acknowledgment), the child will be more likely to repeat the behaviour/s.

Competition

If the child is competitive, the sporting arena (which focuses on competing and winning) may well appeal plus bring out or enhance competitive behaviour. It is important to acknowledge that some people are naturally competitive, and will seek out competition and try their hardest with each event they participate in. It is also true that children can build on their natural competitiveness, particularly if they have parents who value such attributes. Feedback from a driven parent may reinforce the need to train hard and play harder with an emphasis on winning — 'There are no prizes for coming second', 'You don't win the silver; you lose the gold.' If similar behaviours are expressed in different settings (such as at home and on the sports field), a process of generalization has begun. This is where environments that seem similar bring about expressions of similar behaviours — because these behaviours (e.g. pushing oneself) worked in the original setting. As a result, the behaviour can then become firmly entrenched and eventually automatic.

The single-minded focus can also be fostered from an early age by choosing similar-behaving peers and engaging with groups where such an approach is valued. This reinforces particular behaviours and perspectives, and it does this in a selective manner: one whereby similar ways of thinking and behaving are reinforced while diverging approaches are ignored. This effectively selects out certain behaviours, thus maintaining a particular culture for the group. There is often low tolerance within competitive peer groups for individuals not demonstrating effort or achieving at expected levels. Few people, especially at a young age, want to be different so the drive to perform and meet expectations is set up and maintained by social pressures. Fear of ostracism is strong in young people (especially teens) and can therefore make adherence to behavioural expectations a strong driving force. This can see key behaviours such as pushing oneself, prioritizing goals and having high expectations become a 'usual' part of the person's approach to life. This can set some individuals on an eventual course to burnout from an early age. They 'need' to excel at school or sport and then push themselves at university or their early jobs/careers. However, with the fortitude of youth, they can often cope with the initial costs from overdoing things. This of course allows the driven behaviour to operate under the radar and not be detected until some crisis or significant difficulty is encountered (possibly years later).

Controlling life

There are parents whose approach is to control things and maintain an organized life. Such parents can place emphasis on high and potentially unrealistic expectations. However, such expectations are not necessarily in the service of enhancing the child and their needs. Rather, this parenting style emphasizes orderliness and obedience, leaving little room for variability in meeting targets. The consequences of poor performance can be swift, and can teach a lesson about the place and value of one's own needs plus the importance of prioritizing the expected outcome.

One of the biggest problems in this family system is that affirmation can be contingent — that is, dependent on some condition being met, usually upon performance at or above a certain level. Once the standard is met, affection and attention may be offered. Conversely, if the level is not achieved, attention could be withheld or removed. Of potential relevance to the developing child is that affirmation might not be given for anything less than meeting the expected standard. The young person can therefore struggle to develop flexibility in how they respond to life's events. The child unfortunately learns that 'good enough' does not exist or that it is something to avoid at all costs.

Another challenge with such parents is that they might not confine their comments and responses to the child's performance. Unfortunately, they may personalize it in a negative or undermining manner. Thus, the feedback might not be about the task being difficult but more that the child is at fault or that they are unable to produce the goods as expected. As a result, a demanding cycle can be set up whereby the child learns that to be valued (by the most important people to them) they must go about their tasks in a single-minded fashion. If a parent behaves coldly to the child (who has by now picked up that the parent values high effort and perfect outcomes) then the child can end up pushing themselves to both please and achieve. But note that the desire for a positive outcome is related to an external party. There is no intrinsic motivation or self-generated ideal here. Rather, a child (desiring affection and/or attention) is learning to perform in a manner that maximizes the chances they will be acknowledged and/or given some affection.

The delivery of rewards is now contingent upon a particular outcome. Over time, this can shift the perspective ever more firmly in an external direction, whereby one's own needs, tiredness and limits are ignored in pursuit of the achievement. Although the behaviour was originally related directly to obtaining affection, it will morph (over time) into focusing on the goal completion or perfect performance itself. The original aspect of seeking reinforcement has now become wrapped up in ways of behaving to achieve certain goals. Although the parent may no longer be the main driver of such behaviour, parental substitutes — teachers, coaches or employers — can assume the same role. This intermittently reinforces the dedicated focus, high level of performance and non-questioning approach to activity. Finally, the (eventual) major driver of such behaviour becomes the individual themselves. This can see the person internalize the standards and expectations, so that they become their own worst critic and relentlessly drive themselves to achieve.

An amazing first-person account of a powerful work ethic and the effects of early upbringing can be found in the autobiography of former world number one tennis player, Andre Agassi. This honest, insightful but raw account of Agassi's rise to fame provides a personal narrative of many of the factors contained in this book. Agassi details a struggle with standards which were too high and, indeed, unsustainable. These were not developed by him nor were they encountered by chance. Rather, they were proscribed, enforced and reinforced by his father. This myopic parent apparently had a goal to have a child who would not only become a professional tennis player but also number one in the world. In amongst the various challenges, achievements and relationships in the book is a thread that weaves a story of someone who was set up to perform and then shown how to push himself beyond personal limits. It is a first-hand account of what the life of a top-level sportsperson (who operated consistently with a superhuman work ethic) was like from the beginning. It is interesting to read the real-life battles he had with self-criticism (and, at times, self-loathing) and perfectionism. Agassi also describes in vivid terms what this struggle with perfectionism was like: '... perfection isn't the goal in our house, it's the law. If you're not perfect, you're a loser.' Perfectionism can be a central feature of life for someone with a strong work ethic or A/N personality; it will therefore be explored more fully in Chapter 7.

Agassi describes a torturous journey through life, whereby he takes on (reluctantly, yet powerfully) the approach to judgment modelled by his father. At one point he outlines the transition from being the receiver of harsh criticism to becoming a finely tuned purveyor of the same: 'I've internalized my father — his impatience, his perfectionism, his rage — until his voice doesn't just feel like my own, it is my own, I no longer need my father to torture me. From this day on, I can do it all by myself.' This gives us an example of the harsh internal critic that can play a critical role in keeping expectations around high levels of performance firmly in the forefront of the world view of someone with an unremitting work ethic.

BEING UNSURE CAN SHAPE OUR BEHAVIOUR

The developing, hardworking personality comes to realize there is much riding on the outcome of any venture. This can impact on behaviour but also personal confidence levels and decision-making before even beginning something. It can become scary to actually start a task for, once begun, the performance is open to scrutiny by parents, teachers, coaches and employers. Unfortunately, such youngsters start to live and behave within a closed system whereby there appears to be only two possible outcomes from behaviour: success or failure. While this might not be the reality, the developing hardworking personality tends to operate in this manner and therefore can conceive of only these two results. One of these, of course, is more acceptable to the self than the other.

Over time, fear of failure can become associated with the drive to succeed. This developing fear can affect the type and level of behaviours adopted. Plus, the young person may even begin to hold back from starting tasks at all. They might put something off for a long time, often until there is no choice (via pressure from parents, for example, or a school deadline looming) but to get underway. Interestingly, others can view this lack of commencement as tardiness or being 'too laid back'. The issue is perhaps better identified as procrastination and this might not be due to laziness or lack of motivation. Rather, the developing personality is faced with the dilemma that, once started, there is no option but to finish the task in a manner that is acceptable — that is, correct. Those first few paragraphs of a high-school essay become 'real' and therefore a public representation of the individual and what they can or cannot do. At such times, the fear of failure can become so strong that one must knuckle down and complete the task well *or* not go near it.

It would be incorrect to say that the developing person (child, teen, young adult) is comfortable with procrastination. They are more likely to be motivated by negative factors than by positive ones — to avoid failure, poor performance or being put into situations where the sense of self is at risk. Thus, for these people, time can be spent rehashing things so that the task is more or less complete before it is committed to the public arena. One of the traps for such people is that the more times they experience difficulties achieving at the level they believe is expected of them, the greater the fear of potential failure can become.

The developing, internal driving force is to be correct and to meet the expected standard. This is potentially contributed to by a sense of insecurity. The person might not have grown up within a consistent framework where results, responses and affection were always predictable. The background to their development could have been one of high expectations — both external and then, over time, internal. The parenting style they experienced may have involved restricted positive comments. It was therefore the shifting target for gaining approval that perhaps led to insecurity around what is expected or appropriate. The level to be attained may have been unclear or even variable, which meant the child could only conceive of pushing hard/er to try to meet a target that was not specifically identified. An A in the last exam might lead to an expectation of an A+ in the next one, but with no greater level of resulting reinforcement. Acknowledgement from one or both parents might have been hard to obtain at times and approval possibly even more elusive. Without this, the child is at the mercy of external thresholds that can shift, though usually in one direction: upwards. Alongside this, the parent's critical comments are internalized and this can become the predominant internal voice. However, it is now more powerful as it literally cannot be escaped and is also more undermining because it has become the 'self' telling the 'self' how poorly s/he is doing. It is of course a reflection of the critical parent, but it is now someone who can be argued with even less — yourself.

As you have probably deduced from this chapter, not everyone who has self-driving traits came from exactly the same background. They may share some similarities in the factors that contributed to the way they interact with the world. However, it would be wrong to assume that any particular driven individual can be pigeon-holed as coming from one type of background or environment. I recall one client who provided a 'textbook' outline of these mercilessly driven behaviours and the related longer-term impacts upon his personal wellbeing. As my therapist's antenna was triggered by the challenges he described, I offered the possibility that he had been raised in an environment with parents who had high standards and possibly even higher expectations of their children. To this insightful (I thought!) observation, he immediately replied, 'Not at all, Doc, my parents were both hippies; they didn't expect anything of us kids.' He went on to relate how he had consciously decided to establish personal standards, expect highly of himself and also push himself to achieve in reaction to this lack of expectation, structure and modelling. So, there are always variations on a theme. How you came to be living a self-driven or A/N lifestyle might share similarities with a particular description from above or you might relate to components of several of these descriptions. Neither of these is wrong because, as you will see in this book, few things in this world are purely one thing or the other.

To manage this situation, you can benefit from help to explore where the problems came from and how they developed. As part of this, it can be helpful for you, as a driven adult, to realize that the internal pushing might be related to an early lack of acknowledgment and limited affirmation for success at any level other than 'being the best'. You might also benefit from understanding that there actually is such a thing as 'good enough' and that providing an outcome that is 'good enough' is not the lowest level of achievement, nor is it a failure! If there is no change in understanding or ability to manage this relentless pursuit of achievement, the child who becomes the driven adult will continue to judge themselves harshly, feel they are underperforming (unless it is at the extreme end) and continue to push themselves. This can set you on a course that leads, steadily, towards the experience of overperforming, becoming worn out or unwell, and eventually crashing headlong into burnout.

TO SUM UP

We don't tend to suddenly become a highly driven person, nor does it tend to come and go. Granted, we can all become focused on a project but the very focused and directed personality style is longer lasting than this. It possibly comes about in a family context with an orientation to achieving and performing well. The family may also have had at least one parent who demonstrated, via their own behaviour, the way to approach tasks. This modelling can be an important part of our earliest exposure to ways of living that focus on doing and completing.

Related to the this, the way that significant others respond to your early behaviours can shape subsequent choices and actions. If you were praised for certain ways of behaving, you would be more likely to repeat those behaviours. As a result, you perhaps come to expect that doing well and performing to high standards is what is required, or 'usual'. The interesting question (which doesn't often get asked at this stage) is where this might all lead to. One answer, of course, is burnout.

If our early environment was not consistent or we couldn't predict what was required to earn praise, we may have learned to push ourselves in the hope of obtaining positive attention and reinforcement. One result of this is a sense that the outcome — as opposed to the process or effort — is the most important thing. This can become the yardstick for measuring our worth. If, within the family, praise and attention were tethered to high achievement, it is possible that we did not learn that 'good enough' is indeed good enough.

One risk with such a learning experience is that feeling good about your achievement can become externalized to the responses of and affirmations from others. The drive to achieve may have come from a need to please or measure up to the expectations of others. Over time, you may well take on board the pressure to do well and to be seen as good. As much of the developing sense-of-self can depend on levels of achievement, a fear of failure can become a new 'driving' factor for important behaviours and tasks. This can lead to people seeing the world in an either/or manner, whereby we are either meeting the high standards we set ourselves or we are failing.

As the young person (and developing driven personality) has little practice with realistic and fair expectations, the only choice seems to be to push oneself in order to meet the goal/s that have been set. Unfortunately, along with this drive to achieve can come a strong tendency to judge (read: criticize) yourself and your performance.

A chance for change

Developing an understanding of where things come from doesn't mean that blame needs to be assigned. This is not about saying 'This is Mum's/Dad's fault' and then feeling absolved of responsibility. Nor is it about becoming angry at 'them' for doing 'this' to 'me'. Rather, it is more about understanding, learning and realizing why things came about. If you can gain this appreciation, then things might not seem so random and perhaps there is more potential for gaining some control. If you are tempted to apportion blame, remember that one or both of your parents might have exhibited some of these behaviours ... and guess where they might have got them from? Chances are that they picked up their approach to life in much the same way you did — via modelling, reinforcement and shaping of responses to situations.

From this chapter, you have hopefully gained some idea of how your driven approach to life may have developed. If you can also get a handle on what has been maintaining this approach, you might feel in a stronger position to bring about some change. Therefore, the next chapter will consider a range of factors that may have kept the driven and even A/N approach alive for you. Hopefully, if you can gain an understanding of these factors, you might be open to considering whether there are new or different ways of engaging in activities. These new approaches can help you shift from the patterns of behaviour that have become so familiar and may well have led to burnout in your adult life.

TRY THIS

One question to consider as you continue to read this book is whether things have to remain this way forever. Maybe, just maybe, it might be all right to pause and ask yourself if it is okay to start doing things differently. In this vein, complete the following simple statements. You might not come up with any answers immediately, or you might even come up with reasons why this won't work. If so, don't panic. This doesn't mean that considering something new is impossible. Chances are that you are experiencing your mind throwing up the barriers to change. Human minds don't like moving away from the familiar and they can easily generate many reasons for remaining with the status quo. Don't be put off by this; just have another go.

Find a pen and paper and then complete the following sentences in your own words:

If I finished work earlier each night I would be able to …

By having more time with my partner/family, my life would …

When I learn to be less hard on myself, it will be easier to …

Not expecting myself to be perfect will allow me to …

4.
WHAT KEEPS THIS ALL GOING?

As we have seen, there is a flow on from early learning and life experiences through to our behaviour and responses as a young person and then as an adult. This ties together the connections between parenting, family dynamics and expectations as well as the reinforcement paradigms we encounter over time.

These important variables come together in an individual package that is specific to each person. How they are expressed depends on the person, their history, the relevant environment and social situation. These key variables can have a bearing on what professional roles we seek out in adult life and how we behave within them. So your career choice might not be as spontaneous or random as you thought. It is likely that what we bring with us may have a key role in determining how we engage in the tasks required of us. Thus, it might not be what we do but how we do it that is most relevant — particularly as we head towards burnout!

SCHEMAS: YOUR PRE-GOOGLE GUIDANCE SYSTEM

Engagement in activity is not a simple relationship of 'see task, do task'. There is a multitude of variables within you that can come into play. These include your immediate appraisal of the situation and the actual decisions you take. From these aspects, your behaviour will follow; this can be a new or novel approach or an automatic behaviour. Underpinning an automatic behaviour are longstanding and often deeply entrenched determiners of behaviour, also known as *schemas*. These are ways of viewing the world that have been laid down and reinforced over a number of years. In essence, schemas serve as templates to help us make sense of events, plus they impact how we think about and approach our world.

Over time, our schemas affect how we view ourselves, and they impact the types of behaviours we exhibit, as well as our relationships with others. Additionally, they will begin to influence choices around behaviour. Importantly, schemas, once laid down, are very hard to rid ourselves of. The problem, however, might not be that the schemas are present or even activated, but that we put them into action frequently and rigidly. This is of relevance if you are a driven person who tends to (repeatedly and unquestioningly) apply the early messages about effort, achievement and what is required to be 'good' (or should that be perfect?) at something.

One of the most interesting groups of clients I work with is airline pilots. These people tend to be very good at their job, have highly developed problem-solving skills and a longstanding passion for flying. They are also, to a person, perfectionists.

Amir is a pilot who flies international routes and he was referred to me because he had experienced a lowering of his mood, described difficulties switching off from his job

What keeps this all going?

and felt he had lost his passion for flying. After a few quick questions, it was obvious that he was also struggling with a strong dose of imposter syndrome.

Amir was acutely aware of the importance of safety within his industry and he prided himself on being a well-performing pilot. However, in the last year or so he had begun to doubt himself and his abilities. From talking with Amir, I could see that his reflection on his performance had shifted from a positive review of each flight to a self-directed criticism of his role in the cockpit. Without realizing it, Amir was microscopically examining all actions and mapping these against the standard operating procedures. The result was that he found 'mistakes' and 'errors' in each flight. This resulted in Amir monitoring his performance even more closely and worrying about his fitness to perform his duties. He found that he could not stop thinking about each 'mistake' he had made in flight. Interestingly, there had never been any concerns voiced by colleagues or management and he had always passed the simulator tests with very positive feedback.

As we explored the role of schemas together, I could see that Amir had two powerful ones that were ever-present and directed much of his approach to flying. He held himself to very high standards and operated with a strong sense of responsibility. These were perfect schemas to have as a pilot — I'm sure all the travelling public would agree. The difficulty was that Amir had been applying these schemas to such a level that it was essentially impossible for him to live up to his own expectations. The outcome was a sense of not meeting what was required of him (despite a lack of any objective evidence) and an anxious preoccupation around his ability to perform. In the face of this crippling self-scrutiny, Amir (unfairly) began to see himself as not being as capable as he should be when doing what he loved: flying aircraft.

The schemas or core beliefs that driven and A/N people respond to can be around working hard, being the best, looking after others or not showing weakness. They tend to lie dormant until activated by a situation that is familiar, or by a combination of factors and events that conspire to trigger them. (This is much the same process that allows a dormant virus to express itself.) Perhaps a key issue is that, once a schema is kicked into gear, it will open a box that contains familiar and well-rehearsed behaviours. There is an interaction between the person (with all their prior experiences and beliefs) and the situation. However, there tends to be little appraisal of the situation that confronts the person or of the range of options available at the time. Rather, there will usually be a response connected to feelings, thoughts and behaviours the person has previously employed in similar situations. Without the appraisal aspect (where we make sense of things), the relevant schema is automatically implemented and this will continue to be the case in future (similar) events and situations. In fact, how we make sense of a situation (that is, how we appraise it) is directly affected by our personal schemas.

In some ways, schemas act as a sort of shorthand that guides us and almost pre-selects behaviours for particular situations. Think of them as Mother Nature's version of Google Maps: a course of action is put forward without much actual thinking having been applied, and then we follow it. However, without accounting for variations to the situation or suggested route, we can sometimes end up in an environment we are not fully prepared for. This is much like the news reports of hapless travellers who blindly trust their mapping device only to find themselves in the middle of nowhere, up a goat track (unable to reverse down) with snow falling, daylight disappearing and only an already opened can of Coke and half-eaten egg sandwich for company. Not quite what they had planned or expected when they set out on a course of action, and with no real idea of how they ended up in that situation.

It is true that using schemas can be very adaptive and labour saving, but some schemas may not have been developed in the most balanced or nuanced of environments. Thus, they can contain and promote responses that will cost you in the long run. With respect to driven behaviour, the messages we have been given by significant others and the expectations we have taken on board often impact how we view activities, roles and tasks. Our early life events lay the groundwork for schemas, which will then be triggered in situations related to performance. As a result, a person who can't seem to stop working will potentially respond in a manner that follows the script associated with pushing, achieving and doing their best.

Researchers Bamber and McMahon have identified that people can be unconsciously drawn to situations, and therefore employment choices, that will trigger the not-always-helpful schemas they developed early on (e.g. not stopping a task until everything is complete). Additionally, they suggest that certain underlying schemas may actually be a vulnerability factor for developing occupational stress later in life (e.g. burnout). They go on to say that healthcare workers often have strong schemas around caring for others, which may have begun as a way to gain approval in the family environment. Or they may have been given roles early on where they were required to care for younger siblings. This 'self-sacrifice' schema is identified as eventually coming at the cost of not prioritizing or meeting their own needs.

Bamber and McMahon also give examples of another early schema associated with perfectionistic behaviours and the drive to meet high personal standards. They relate this type of schema to growing up in an environment with strong and relatively inflexible parental and familial expectations. This supports the ideas put forward in this book. One of the most interesting aspects of this research is that, while unhelpful schemas can sometimes have a negative impact as you live with them, they may also be central to your ability to perform in a quality manner. The writers go on to offer the seemingly ironic viewpoint that these same (potentially unhelpful) ways of interacting with the world may actually have positive spin-offs for the organization, industry or sporting worlds that the individual engages in. A real-life example of this is illustrated in the case study of Amir on p. 45. Thus, the needs of the individual might not be met (over time) but the needs of the group or organization may well be met or exceeded.

To make gains and positive changes in your life, it will help to learn to account for what is happening behind the scenes. It is not enough to just identify the unhelpful behaviours (e.g. consistently working long hours or redoing work to achieve perfection). Change will only be enduring if you can learn about the schemas that are pushing you to act in potentially unhelpful and/or unhealthy ways. By understanding and formulating what is behind rigidly enacted behaviours (plus the costs attached), there is more chance you can understand and see merit in the effort required to bring about change ... and then sustain it.

Schemas: some examples

Some examples of schema-related themes that can make you vulnerable to developing burnout include:

- expecting/chasing perfection
- prioritization of work tasks is important
- responsibility is central to doing well
- failure is to be avoided at all costs
- being hard on yourself is needed to get anywhere
- a strong work ethic defines who you are
- success comes from total/complete application
- other people's needs are more important than your own
- others will judge you if you don't perform properly
- you're not qualified/experienced enough for your job/position.

The chances are, if you are someone who regularly overdoes activity, pushes beyond your tolerance levels or tries to do the best for your employer or client (despite the cost to yourself), you will be responding to one or more of the schemas listed above. However, the way to make positive change is not to try to undo or eliminate the schemas. It is to learn to identify which ones you have operating. This involves knowing what they look and feel like when they are activated, plus consciously considering your options before enacting them. Of course, schemas can bring about high levels of positive outcome — for example, completing tasks and achieving goals. However, they can also work against us and result in negative experiences, particularly over time, as they are repeatedly activated and expressed.

Your personal schemas are like the ingredients in a recipe, whereby they have an effect on the taste or 'outcome' of the completed dish. Imagine you are renowned for a special soup that your friends and family are always keen to have at your dinner parties. As you prepare the soup, you use the same ingredients as always, in order to get that much-sought-after taste. However, if during the preparation your partner knocks your arm just as you are adding the secret chilli powder, the taste experience will be quite different for your guests. It is not a change to the ingredients that has altered the taste, it is the amount of one ingredient — which then alters the overall taste sensation. The ingredients remain the same, the number of ingredients is the same but the *amount* of one is different, and this significantly impacts the outcome. Think of your schemas in the same way, where they are consistently present and have an effect on how you behave and interact. Now, if one of these schemas (e.g. a strong work ethic) gets powerfully triggered and you automatically follow its direction, the balance of your workplace 'soup' is going to be dominated by one contributor. This will have a disproportionate effect on the resulting behaviour, which is directed by that one schema and its attributes.

PERSONALITY STYLE: THE 'YOU' AND HOW YOU SHOW THIS

It is important not to make the mistake of relating to personality styles — that is, the way you action or demonstrate the elements of who you are — as being complete and total. It can be more helpful to understand that the consistently hard-working person experiencing burnout might have many strengths and weaknesses and that these can, in turn, be comprised of a range of 'sub-species'. An important element is the tendency to be conscientious, which the industrial and organizational psychology literature identifies

What keeps this all going?

as a key variable related to performance with tasks. However, it may well be that there are also sub-components to this important aspect. We should therefore ask what makes up this conscientious behaviour. If you can identify these aspects, there may be more opportunity to finetune the impact and expression of this. Some of the key ingredients within this conscientious approach to work life include a sense of duty, an all-encompassing orientation towards achievement, and of course some pretty strong willpower or self-discipline. By accounting for these factors, you may be able to bring about a more fine-grained analysis of your life, patterns of behaviour and repeated actions, which, in turn, can offer more specific targets for change and modification.

It is possible that, by the decisions taken and behaviours expressed, you could be shaping your world to some extent. The personality style you bring to the workplace may well promote particular behaviours and ways of engaging in relationships. Evidence of this can be seen in choices of specialty areas in the medical world. Any patient who has undergone surgery can readily tell you there is a plain and obvious difference in personality and 'bedside manner' between the family doctor, the anaesthetist and the surgeon (ever tried getting one of the latter to converse with you for more than six minutes?). It is also true that people who like to push themselves and value achievement are seldom likely to undertake roles where goals are easily met and provide no challenge. This is as valid in the sporting and artistic fields as it is in the business world. By choosing jobs that fit their personal disposition, a person may demonstrate greater job performance (they like it, so they will do more) and this will probably lead to job-related success. However, it can also lead to doing too much for too long and bringing about the burnout we are exploring together.

It is, of course, too simplistic to say that personality style drives everything. In terms of job performance, there may well be an interaction between personality style, the job chosen, workplace setting, any training or education you receive, and general environmental factors associated with your world. The question, of course, is whether you can alter a key 'ingredient', eliminate it (or its effect), or perhaps attempt to provide ways of softening the way it is experienced. Thus, with personality styles, the goal is not to eliminate a certain aspect but rather to learn how much (and when) to dial it up or down. This is based on the fact that aspects of personality are not entirely positive or entirely negative; perhaps the degree, frequency and strength with which they are expressed may be more relevant.

Understanding yourself

Rather than attempting a 'personality-ectomy', it might be best to understand where your specific vulnerabilities are, to be able to recognize when your schemas are becoming active and know how to manage or mitigate their effect. Potentially, greater change and gains can be brought about by understanding (and working with) your personality style. Key to helping this become acceptable is to realize that having a strong and goal-focused personality style is not wrong. Rather, it is about understanding the at-times problematic aspects and identifying why it might be useful to be able to modify the impact of the behaviours that follow. This can offer a useful outline or framework from where you can begin to make changes — not 'all or nothing' change but, rather, a finetuning that might provide benefits to you, your health and career.

INTOLERANCE OF UNCERTAINTY

Some driven people have come from an environment characterized by not knowing what is expected of them, and therefore may find it difficult to tolerate ill-defined events and situations. Perfectionists and A/N people, for example, prefer to know what is expected, how to participate and also (possibly, most importantly) what the threshold is for achievement. How does one set one's sights or apportion energy if the requirements are not outlined? Being unsure about things can lead to a person interpreting such situations as threatening. Indeed, ambiguity can be a scary place for the A/N or driven person to be. This lack of clarity can potentially set up a sense of dread, particularly around the potential for performing poorly. The chances of failure may realistically be low but, unfortunately, the actual probabilities are not always identified in a realistic manner.

Intolerance of uncertainty is essentially a way of viewing the world and, more specifically, events that are personally important. The individual develops or maintains a sort of bias in the way they view things — with an emphasis on the negative. This involves relating to current or future events as potentially threatening, even if there is no clear evidence that things will go wrong. As a result, the person can start to behave in ways that, they hope, might reduce this uncertainty. They may seek increasing amounts of detail from others (e.g. supervisors or colleagues) as a way of bringing about the desired or 'needed' clarity. This is aimed at making themselves feel safer and more confident by attempting to impose some structure on events. However, it can have unintended negative effects; for example, within the workplace, people can view your reassurance-seeking as an admission of inability.

Encountering uncertainty is a multidimensional experience. It involves cognitive, emotional and behavioural responses to the uncertainty, all of which are characterized by an unpleasant, gnawing sensation. Remember that some people who relentlessly push themselves have been striving for a long time to be in control of situations. When faced with uncertainty, the sense of self is at risk and the person may start to feel vulnerable. Unfortunately, this can be interpreted within oneself as weakness (harsh internal critic, anyone?), which of course can be further threatening to personal identity. Within this context, the unsure person may respond in a manner that biases interpretations and general processing towards the worst-case scenario. Consider what this is like if your role is to make policy decisions or offer advice to other departments within an organization!

It is perhaps not hard to see how this difficulty with tolerating uncertainty develops on the road to burnout. In essence, uncertainty relates to the potential for things to go wrong (e.g. poor outcomes) — this clashes with the internal image, and demands that the person be in control and always achieving. Coupled with a harsh inner critic, such a self-image can cause a degree of dissonance: key things about the self do not fit together too well. Negative, anticipatory concerns therefore clash with the positive, 'in control' self-perception that usually drives the person towards achievement. Both perfectionism and the tendency to overthink things can then lead to 'paralysis by analysis', where the person struggles to think clearly, make decisions or take action due to an overfocus on detail or certain facets of a task. This results in the person feeling as though they can't function (or function to the expected standard) when faced with uncertainty. This can become an even greater issue if deadlines are looming and strict.

It has been suggested that intolerance of uncertainty may be most apparent and relevant in relation to environments of core concern. While you might be struggling generally to tolerate uncertainty, this can become even more pronounced in, for example, the office or boardroom. Overestimating the potential for negative outcomes can become a major problem when operating at high levels of responsibility, where peak performance is central to maintaining your standards and position. A key issue here is the negative estimation. Unfortunately, over time, this way of viewing situations can become an automatic process, which makes it hard to identify and therefore manage. Once this process is set in train, it flows towards the internal perfection driver and starts to raise personal concerns about (self) performance and therefore outcome. The internal critic then comes in to bat and may well change the course and direction of the game. Initially, this might mean a doubling of effort to overcome the perceived challenges, but it may also lead to a fear of failure taking over and impacting the chosen responses. The issue to grasp here is that there might actually be no real basis for the threatening view. Therefore, the negative tailspin that eventuates might be unnecessary and confidence levels might also be unnecessarily affected. When all this is operating, you might become 'paralyzed' due to the uncertainty, so that you find it hard to make decisions or put relevant actions into place. Thus, a previously decisive and efficient person may well find they can no longer perform in the manner accustomed or expected. If you are someone the team looks to for direction and decision-making, such hesitation might become obvious and impact team morale and trust. This challenging scenario is even more likely when the effects of burnout are starting to take hold of an individual.

But what if you could learn that uncertainty is not a portent of doom? What if you could see it as something you can tolerate and even manage? The outcome would be the chance to continue succeeding, which might also help stave off some of the unhelpful self-doubts that can eat away at you and enhance the feelings of burnout.

TO SUM UP

As this chapter has made clear, there are thinking processes that happen before a behaviour or activity occurs. The pattern looks like this:

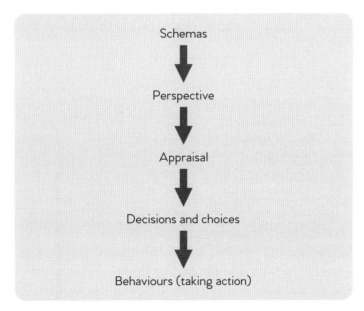

Despite these thinking processes being intangible, they are nevertheless real and are key components to how things develop. Generally, we can easily notice the final phase of taking action. However, the steps prior to this are what orient you and prime you to respond in certain ways. Importantly, we can now see that the perspective you bring to a situation will direct the flow of traffic, so to speak. The next step is appraisal, or how we make sense of what is in front of us at any given time. Both these aspects can be influenced by a range of things, such as mood state or environmental demands. The other aspect we are now aware of is the role of schemas, which may lie underneath (and wrap around) these processes and consistently influence them. Thus, to truly bring about a better understanding of what is driving a behaviour (e.g. working relentlessly) we need to take account of all these factors.

Schemas provide us with a shorthand way for making sense of the world. They develop within our early personal environment and influence how we interact with the world. However, problems stem from how we put schemas into practice. We tend to run with them without thinking, due to the fact they are so familiar. One result of this is that we repeatedly use the same responses to situations and may rigidly follow the 'guidelines' offered by the schemas. However, if we can become more flexible in how we make sense of situations and explore options for responding, we will have a better chance of adapting to tasks.

If you overwork, any lack of clarity can be a scary zone to be playing around in. Uncertainty is seen as threatening and therefore something to be avoided, but real-life experience shows us that this is not always possible. The feelings of threat can lead to a reduced sense of confidence and tug at the need for perfection, while simultaneously undermining the sense of self. Unfortunately, over time, uncertainty in life can affect how a person relates to their role, colleagues and specific tasks. This changed approach is characterized by a negative estimation of the threat value, resulting in the risks being over-identified — which in turn can lead to a triggering of the fear of failure.

A chance for change

Difficulties tolerating uncertainty revolve around worry about the future, so it can help to become more comfortable with the 'here and now'. What might life be like if you learned to adopt more of a 'wait and see' attitude, rather than chasing the goal of wanting to control every uncertain situation? You might find it becomes easier to live in a space where not everything is predictable, for, in essence, isn't this what life is actually like? One key aspect to making a change like this is to view problems and setbacks as simply a normal part of life. Now here's a bit of a mind-spin for you: what if these uncertain situations could be viewed as opportunities to learn from, to refine your technique, or to develop new ways of approaching a task?

There can be a strong drive to avoid uncertain situations. However, you may have gathered already that such avoidance does not teach you anything about managing either the situations themselves or the associated feelings. One approach to help address this is to consciously put yourself in situations where you start to feel uncertain and therefore uncomfortable. '*What?*' I hear you scream. I am, in effect, suggesting you be bold and do something really scary ... such as being spontaneous! Consider doing something on the spur of the moment — radical, I know. This doesn't have to be a major task or accomplishment; it can be heading out to buy something (unplanned) for dinner, going out to visit something or someone (not tomorrow or next week, but *today*), sitting down to listen to your favourite music this afternoon (just because you like it) or going for a drive to the beach or park (for no reason other than the weather is nice). Try to incorporate such spontaneity into your life on a more regular basis.

The aim is to confront and open yourself up to situations that will provoke a sense of uncertainty. Show yourself that there doesn't always need to be a reason or goal associated with doing things. The risks are small with such tasks but they will still bring about feelings of uncertainty (partly because there is no script and therefore no predictable outcome), and if you face these feelings you are on the way to overcoming them. If you like, gently and gradually extend the level and type of spontaneity to differing domains in your life. This will expose you (in a controlled manner, with few major consequences) to the discomfort and will help inoculate you to the unsettling impact of the emotional responses, such as feeling exposed and out of control.

To assist with the long-standing need for predictability, it can help to become more accepting of the feelings associated with uncertainty. Part of this is to realize that such feelings are essentially unavoidable and are, for the most part, harmless (uncomfortable, for sure, but still harmless). First, though, you will need to know when you are experiencing these feelings of uncertainty and become aware of the unhelpful thoughts and feelings that accompany them. Try the following simple exercise, for which you'll need a pen and paper.

TRY THIS

Think about a role or task that you were unexpectedly asked to complete by someone such as a supervisor or boss, your coach at training or your best friend in a social setting. Take yourself back to the moment you were asked to do this and think about what began to run through your mind ... what were the very first thoughts? These are not the detailed appraisal or risk analysis you might have performed later on, but your immediate thoughts upon hearing the task described. What do you recall about how you began to feel (emotionally and physically) in those first few seconds and minutes? Now write down those thoughts, physical sensations and emotional feelings. What do you notice about them? How would you describe the 'flavour' of these thoughts and feelings? Is there a theme running through them?

If you notice that the feelings and thoughts relate to being unsure (about your ability, for example, or the outcome, or what people might think of you), have another go at the task but use a different scenario and see if the patterns repeat themselves. This of course requires you to be honest with yourself about the thoughts and feelings. Remember, there is no one to impress here, only a person being open to identifying patterns and possibly learning how to deal with aspects that may be keeping fears and concerns alive. If being anxious or unsure is the theme, then revisit each of your scenarios. However, this time, focus on breathing calmly in a relaxed manner and allow yourself to see that these feelings and thoughts can be tolerated and they don't have to result in avoidance or poor performance.

What keeps this all going?

To end this chapter, reflect on the following words of wisdom:

Ain't no use worrying about things beyond your control,
Because if they're beyond your control, ain't no use worrying ...
Ain't no use worrying about things within your control,
Because if you have them under control, ain't no use worrying.

— Mickey Rivers, American former baseball player

5.
TURNING THE TIDE

'I know that I need to change, but I don't have time to.'
EMILY, 38, BUSINESS OWNER

The earlier sections of this book were important. To deal with something or lessen its impact, you first need to know what it is, what it looks like and how it impacts your world. I'm guessing that your lived experience has allowed you to relate and connect with the content already covered. However, we aren't just going to leave things there. As the title of this chapter suggests, it is now time to look at the key issues around you, your burnout experience and what you can do to move forward. The quote above encapsulates some relevant issues around burnout: a desire to change but a feeling that there are things that will prevent this from happening. It also brings to the fore an example of the traps we can experience or perceive as being present.

The fact you are reading this book probably means you are a self-aware individual and have an interest in self-help and self-reflection. It is by this latter (honest) approach that each of us can grasp where our strengths and vulnerabilities are with respect to burnout. As I have suggested, there are undoubtedly significant contributing factors in the workplace(s) you have been operating within. However, there are also parts of 'you' that have had a hand in the development of burnout. If you can identify these aspects, know what they look like and then work to find a better balance or keep them within acceptable and workable limits, you will have a much better chance of not stumbling into the grip of burnout again. The place you have been or often see looming in front of you (unremitting burnout) is, quite simply, not a nice situation to be in. So hopefully you are ready to change things for the better.

Now is the time to take back some control in your life and its direction. Now is the time to realize that it is okay to take care of yourself, and begin to do that. Recent priorities have most likely moved you away from a place that feels comfortable and allows you to do 'you'. I am going to encourage you to account for yourself, your needs and personal values. This is a bit of a voyage of discovery in some ways. For, if you don't see the relevance and reality of your own needs, you run the risk of always placing other people and work demands ahead of yourself. To break this cycle, you will benefit from honouring who you are and relating more consistently to what is important to you. As a way of bringing this front and centre for you, we shall explore key concepts such as personal identity and values.

What might life look like for you if you begin to peel back the layers of burnout and distance yourself from the negative feelings and lack of energy? Well, it could look like it used to (before the trip towards burnout) or it could look similar but different. The choice can be yours if you are open to change and picking up knowledge plus skills to help you on that path. It is possible that you have tried a range of techniques and approaches to help yourself and some of these may have been, overall, less than positive. This might have included the use of alcohol, smoking, drugs, gambling or just pulling back from the world. While it is understandable that you might have tried these options, please understand that they are only ways of avoiding the unpleasant parts of burnout (e.g. strong negative feelings, thoughts and memories). Where we want to head now is towards a repertoire of helpful, workable strategies and approaches.

Being unsure of what lies ahead can breed doubt. When you are starting out with new approaches, this doubt might show up as unhelpful comments about it being too hard to learn new skills or make changes. Don't be put off by this. Rather, remind yourself that the new skills are your key to managing the unpleasant and overwhelming experiences that have come with burnout. By using these strategies, you are placing yourself in the best position to increase your tolerance for uncertainty, and dampening the unpleasant effects that might have directed your life to date.

TURNING STRATEGIES INTO ACTION

Knowing something is not the same as changing something. As behavioural psychologist William Fordyce once said, 'Information is to behaviour change as spaghetti is to a brick.' Think about that for a moment. He is saying that there is essentially no relationship between these variables. As such, he has tapped into an important issue for us: we need to find a way to translate the knowledge about strategies into action. This comes from practice, discipline and application. These are the foundations of a bridge between knowledge and change.

Obtaining positive outcomes from the following sections will come from attempting the exercises outlined. Going over these skills is no different to practising your golf swing or repeating the new steps from dance class. The repetition helps bring confidence in their use and offers the chance to refine your technique. This means that it will be easier to access the relevant skill when you need it most. Waiting for change is not an empowering option. The sign I have in my clinic waiting room reads 'Nothing changes if nothing changes.' Believe this and do something about it!

You don't need to become an expert on all the knowledge, skills and approaches contained in the following sections. You might find that some resonate more with you than others. This is okay. However, I suggest you try them all out, to see what their 'fit' might be like. Then add to your toolbox whatever feels best for you.

Depending on where you are in your journey with burnout, you might need to take some time off of work. This could be a proactive response if you have become aware of burnout's developing effects on you. Unfortunately, for many of my clients, by the time we meet they have either taken extended sick leave or left their job. Part of my hope for this book is that it might help you avoid having to do the latter, as a first-line strategy. I do think there are positive effects from taking a break and giving yourself the chance to rest up. However, I want to make the point that either having a holiday or taking sick leave will not, by themselves, 'fix' things for you. Undoubtedly, having a rest and a chance to de-stress will be beneficial. Unfortunately, if you return to the same workplace, with the same demands and have no new understanding or skills to help yourself, it is unlikely your recovery will continue. This is a little like taking the run-down battery out of your car and leaving it on the garage bench for a week and then hoping it will have recharged itself and have enough new energy to perform the usual tasks required of it. Doesn't sound too likely, does it? Therefore, I strongly encourage you to explore the following sections of this book and add the positive skills to the rest you are planning or taking from your employment role.

THE CHOICE POINT

To help you get into the right headspace to embark on the steps through and beyond burnout, I would like to introduce you to a concept known as the 'choice point'. This is something I picked up from a workshop taught by Dr Russ Harris and I have found it to be very helpful with clients looking to start the process of change. The major plus of this approach is becoming aware that you have a choice in how you behave. This is important as you look to leave behind burnout and try to resist the invitation to slide back into the behaviours that took you there in the first place.

The choice here is between behaviours that will take you *towards* the place/state that you wish to operate in, or those that will take you *away* from that desired space. Your immediate aim is to notice that you can respond to situations with a range of behaviours which fall into two broad camps — those that will help you achieve your aim or those that hinder you in this process. If your desired outcome is to have better balance in your world as you return to work, you have a choice: you can choose behaviours that increase your chances of doing this sustainably, or choose behaviours that make it more likely you don't move in this newly preferred direction. See the example below to grasp how the behaviours on the left-hand side will take you away from your goal, while those on the right-hand side will take you towards this. The 'choice point' is in the box below — this is the moment when you are beginning the return-to-work process. This is when/where you can choose which behaviours to implement and follow.

Turning the tide

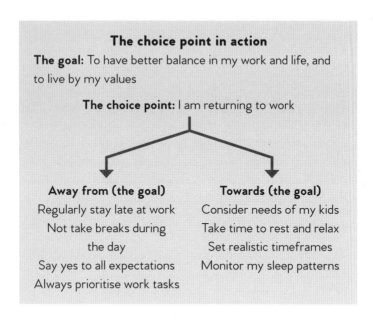

PUSHY THOUGHTS: ACKNOWLEDGE, ACCEPT AND ACCOMMODATE

With increased processing of strong emotions, there is less energy for more useful and adaptive responses to the actual problem at hand. As you become wrapped up in negative thoughts ('I have no option') and feelings (anxiety, sadness, fear), you can start to struggle with the extent of these feelings. You may also find it hard to shift your focus to what is needed (here and now) to bring about a positive resolution. This can be the reality of that gradual descent into burnout, as work demands take over and leave you struggling to make sense of it all. A helpful strategy is to learn to tolerate feelings and thoughts that either drive you beyond your tolerance levels or promote a sense that you need to give up on a task. If you can learn to tone down the strong and demanding thoughts and feelings, you can potentially engage in more effective problem-solving.

Being open to, and not fighting, the uncomfortable feelings can help you to resist the need to keep doing what you have always done. One way to increase your tolerance is to make room for the thoughts and feelings that come up when you encounter a demanding situation. By not fighting these normal responses and not trying to send them packing, you are exposing yourself to the experience and this can help dampen the effects plus lower the sense of threat.

Tolerating feelings is not about giving in to them, nor is it fearing them. By becoming more comfortable with their presence, you can lessen their impact and limit their effects on you and your life. Fighting, running from and struggling with feelings/thoughts will only tire you out and make you more likely to encounter difficulties with worry and anxiety. To be clear, though, tolerating or sitting with feelings and thoughts doesn't mean you have to like or want them. It is about accommodating their presence and minimizing their effects on your life.

One school of therapy that has some direct relevance here is ACT (Acceptance and Commitment Therapy). It offers a range of useful skills and approaches that can be used to assist you to shift towards tolerating and working with these human responses. I use the word 'shift' advisedly; talking about change can feel threatening — almost as though you have been doing things wrong. Shifting is about moving from the place you currently are, so that you can adjust your relationship to the experiences.

Some of the strategies employed in ACT use mindfulness skills to help you defuse from the thoughts, feelings and memories that may be challenging you or keeping you stuck in the negative relationship. Learning to let go of the struggle involves making

Turning the tide

room for the reality of your emotionally driven responses. It is about letting those feelings and concerns be present. Let go of the judgment by labelling the experiences, for example 'I am feeling scared', 'I don't understand what is happening here'. Anything that has a name just has to be less scary.

Mindfulness, or being in the 'now', can help us to sit with, be present alongside and be calmer amongst the distress. As a result, we can reduce the 'noise' from the heightened emotional responses and busy thoughts. This can then allow us to make sense of the situation without the automatic and primed responses that usually encourage us to just carry on or agree to a request.

Approaches that can help us to accept (i.e. make room for) the presence of the feelings and thoughts can include actively deciding to not automatically respond as you have before (e.g. worrying and ruminating). Mindfully being aware (i.e. not being judgmental) of what you are thinking or how you are interpreting a situation will enhance your ability to choose the most useful response.

ACT would suggest that the above outcomes can be achieved by using skills that allow you to contact the present moment, such as being aware of what is happening immediately around you. Try these options:

- Pay close attention to your breathing. Gently breathe in and picture breathing 'around' wherever you physically experience tension associated with mental discomfort. Notice your breathing and what happens in your body as you engage in this. This helps to 'make room' for the sensations, as opposed to trying to eliminate them.
- Let the feelings be present. Don't judge them, just notice them and let them be there. You can observe things without having to engage with them. Think

about a naturalist you might have seen on a TV wildlife program: they observe the animals, take note of what they are doing but do not intervene or try to change their behaviours. As a result, the animals can become used to their presence and not see the naturalist as a threat.
- Allow yourself to be human with your reactions. Tell yourself that many people feel upset, confused and possibly overwhelmed. Be kind to yourself, understand you are being like others and pull back from the urge to judge and fight the sensations.
- Take note of several items in your immediate vicinity, one after the other. Describe them to yourself in detail and really focus on them, as opposed to the feelings you are having about the situation you have encountered. This pulls the brain back from making a 'knee jerk' decision about the current situation.

Each of the above strategies will help you to be more accommodating to the presence of uncomfortable feelings. Over time, this will help you become more able to sit with their presence and not have them push you in a direction that, as you are starting to see, history has shown not to be the most beneficial for you.

ENHANCING CONTROL WHEN IT SEEMS TO HAVE SLIPPED AWAY

I would like to talk about control and what it might have come to mean to you. We saw earlier that one of the precursors of burnout is being in a work environment where you have little to no say on your work tasks (either the type or amount of tasks, or both). The result can be that you feel you have no control and are obliged to perform as required, despite a lack of resources or sense of being able to change things. Additionally, the need to have control over all aspects of your environment and role can also be a factor in developing burnout. This includes what is done and how it is undertaken. Although that may sound preferable to the first point, it comes with its own problems, namely the internal pressure to stay on top of things and the associated feelings that disaster will ensue if you are not directing everything. Finally, issues of helplessness (from not having a sense of control) can arise once burnout has taken hold, plus a desire to re-establish control when your life feels chaotic and overwhelming. The latter can be a positive shift but it can also represent a strong and unclearly directed attempt to grasp any form of control. As you might guess from reading this paragraph, none of these responses is all that helpful. I would like to therefore offer a perspective on control that might help you adjust your relationship with it and perhaps be able to benefit from a functional use of appropriate levels of control.

Being in control is a thorny issue for many people, as they tend to relate to control as being an absolute: you either have complete control or you have none. However, my perspective is that control can be variable, without leaving a person exposed or vulnerable. If you pressure yourself to have complete control, you risk viewing yourself as a failure, and seeing that challenges cannot be managed. It will therefore be helpful for us to explore some aspects of control. Having a workable level of control is about knowing your limits with this variable. If you can learn where and when it is useful to apply yourself and your energy, you might be better placed to manage developing challenges such as burnout.

Paradoxically, by letting go of the (sometimes desperate) need to control everything, you can bring a sense of self-efficacy back to your world. One that may have been characterized by a 'need' to control all aspects of your work and, more recently, attempts to shake off the negative experiences of burnout. It is now time to make a shift on this dimension of control. This is from the absolute to a more realistic, achievable level of working with and effectively organizing your tasks. The simple (but real) starting point of knowing you cannot control everything can be liberating. Once you shift your focus from the pressure to be on top of everything, there is a better chance that your life can become more meaningful and less agitated. The effort to understand, control and direct all things you come across has essentially been a way to bring a sense of safety to your existence. This safety comes from predictability — which is what you have been trying to impose on the uncertain aspects of your world as you slipped towards burnout. The liberating aspect comes from taking pressure off yourself to be in control of everything, all the time. The weight of the expectations around being 'in charge' and knowing what to do in every situation can be unbearable.

Things you can't change — and things you can

A helpful model of control has been proposed by author, educator and businessman Stephen Covey. He talks about there being two important spheres, or circles, in our lives that we need to understand and learn to work with. The first circle contains all the things we are concerned about. These can be many and varied but can include big issues like the planet heating up and the climate changing irrevocably. They can also include the many aspects of your professional role and the behaviours of others within your workplace. Your list might have some similarities to mine, but it is unlikely that it would be exactly the same. What Covey suggests is that we need to grasp the truth that there is probably not much we can do about many of the things on our list — because we (as individuals) do not have any influence over them. What follows from this is that, if we invest a lot of time or energy on these concerns, we will deplete our reserves and lose those resources to use on other issues.

Things that might concern most of us (at one time or another):
- the weather
- climate change
- government policies and decisions
- the state of the economy
- taxation levels
- what other people think of us.

The second circle Covey describes is the circle of influence. This includes the things you can do something about — as opposed to all the bigger picture aspects described above, where you cannot effect any change. If your attention and energy is directed to this smaller — but more relevant — circle, you will have a better chance of bringing about some alteration of the event. This is more efficient and effective, as you are channelling your efforts into things that can be altered by yourself and your efforts. A key element here is the realistic appraisal of what/who is in your circle of influence. If you (erroneously) consider it to be larger/wider than it is, you will be ineffective with your efforts to make change, and drain your personal resources.

Notice the phrase 'circle of influence' — it is not called 'the circle of absolute and total control'. As we have already mentioned, control can be a dimensional thing.

Examples of things you can influence:
- your choices and actions
- how you spend your money
- programs you watch on TV
- the type and frequency of exercise you do
- things you agree to do
- being productive (or not) in your job
- what you eat and when.

The relevance of Stephen Covey's model to burnout is that there are numerous things we are unsure about, which can trigger feelings of angst and concern. You may be motivated to find answers or seek closure in order to settle the disquiet and discomfort you are experiencing. This could see you trying to address issues that you do not (and cannot) have control over, with resulting increases in distress and frustration. It is better for your sense of wellbeing (plus self-efficacy) to target and work on the issues/events that you *can* do something about. You will then be employing your abilities to bring about some increased sense of control, even when your sense of threat is screaming at you that the sky is about to fall in. If you respond via a clear understanding that something is within your control to influence, you will be acting in a problem-solving manner, as opposed to being driven by negative or scary thoughts and feelings.

Do you always need to be in control?

Another aspect of control to consider is that we don't need to always be in control. Nor do we have to have all the answers. At times, it might be useful to try letting go of things. I am not advocating giving in. Rather, consider minimizing your stress and the internal pressure to find a quick response or to 'fix things'. If you cannot problem-solve your way through a certain issue at work, try to identify aspects that you *can* influence. These might include your emotional reactions or unhelpful thoughts about the situation. You might also be able to adjust your perspective about what you are encountering, from overwhelming and threatening to problematic and challenging.

Take a decision to cease trying to deal with things you cannot sort out and focus instead on what you can impact. By dwelling on the uncertainty and how bad things seem for you, you run the risk of your efforts becoming counterproductive. This may just key you in deeper and deeper to what is 'wrong'. Releasing yourself from the unhelpful and ineffective ways of dealing with things can be liberating and enlightening. What about taking the time you would have spent on circular, distressing efforts and shifting this towards more of a focus on what is within your sphere of influence? Just because you cannot make the uncertain certain, does not mean you cannot do anything in a given situation.

If we can't directly target the situation, we can still work with how we are making sense of things and our resultant thoughts and feelings. Working to dampen the pressure from these factors can help us to feel less overwhelmed. If we can acknowledge our cognitive and physical responses, we can stop fighting them or giving in to them. This is about making room for these experiences — showing ourselves that they are real and present, but that they do not have to direct how we respond. In fact, we can do things *despite* having unpleasant feelings and thoughts.

> **TRY THIS**
>
> Take a few minutes to recall a situation where you experienced some significant stress at work. Notice what this felt like for you. Tap into the feelings and thoughts that accompanied that situation. Now, what is happening for you as you recall this experience? Do you feel as if things are getting beyond you or that you can't do anything to help yourself? In a journal or on a piece of paper, write these thoughts and feelings below:
>
> Physical feelings: What are they like? Where are they experienced?
>
> Thoughts: Briefly describe what these are about and what your mind is saying to you.

Often, the above feelings and thoughts are not nice or useful. Indeed, they may be unhelpful and push to the front of your mind the thought that you cannot do anything in the face of the problem. However, what if this is untrue and your mind is slipping into that absolute, either/or way of viewing things? This is dangerous for your confidence and self-control. Let's show you that it is possible to have some control *despite* what is happening to you and for you.

Notice the thoughts and feelings you described above and tap into their experience once again. After you have connected with them, try the following:

- Get up and move. Walk across the room. Touch the far wall.
- Turn around and walk back to your seat.
- Now, choose whether you want to sit down again in the same spot or shift to a different place and then sit there.

'So what?' I hear you say. Well, you have just exerted some control in the face of upsetting and unpleasant thoughts and feelings. You didn't need to get rid of them or completely solve the issue before you were able to do something. You made room for the feelings and thoughts — and then did things anyway.

Perhaps try this activity once or twice every day until you get the hang of it. Then, when the unwanted feelings show up in the face of those demands at work, you will be able to demonstrate to yourself that you can do something — that is, that you have some control.

Remember, control isn't about absolutes. Nor is it only about big issues. You can have some control over your day-to-day life by establishing routines and having some structure. This can be as simple as setting a regular time to get up each day. You can choose to do things as opposed to slavishly following what you think is expected of you. This brings about and reinforces a sense of personal agency. By doing this, you are targeting things within your circle of influence and it helps set up the experience of achievement. This is the art of building up your sense of self-efficacy as well. If you know that you can organize your day and exert some influence over aspects of your life, this will help with those feelings of being overwhelmed by the demands of work. Knowing you can do some stuff can ease the fear that other things are beyond you or too big for you to address. The beauty of this is that you can approach the world and know that, even though some things are unclear and uncertain, there are actions you can take to influence aspects of your world plus show yourself that you can be an active player in your own life.

YOUR SPHERE OF RESPONSIBILITY

This involves a rather neat, but unhelpful nexus between a schema and some internal language. The particular schema involves having high levels of responsibility and is one I often see in clients suffering with burnout. The language used when this schema is operating consists of those imperatives that make it obvious to you that there is no option, e.g. 'I must', 'I need to', 'I have to', 'I've got to'. Sound familiar? These co-conspirators can set in motion a challenging and potentially frenetic dance that you get caught up in. They take the lead and set the pace — you follow blindly, automatically fitting in with the direction they take you.

As we already know, schemas are powerful templates that were laid down over time. They bring about automatic and non-critical responding — in line with the learned message. Having an overly developed sense of responsibility regularly shows up in burnout, particularly with conscientious or perfectionistic people. The accepted message is that you take on what is given or suggested and ensure that *all* tasks within that sphere of responsibility are done correctly and in a timely manner. The language promotes the non-critical appraisal of what is required ('I must complete this'). One of the other things we have learned about people experiencing burnout is that they struggle with perspective. Thus, what is or isn't yours to do can become a fuzzy concept. The way people often deal with this uncertainty is to turn it into a certainty (i.e. 'that's all mine and I better get it sorted'). Although this will invariably add to your workload and increase your stress levels, having some certainty is sort of, maybe, almost, like a plan! As a result of this keenness (or slavish response) to the schema, you will find that your sphere of responsibility tends to grow. It gets filled up with new tasks, different expectations or an additional role — or two. Once the perfection driver kicks in, you might end up taking over other people's tasks or roles as you consider they might not be up to the required standard or 'won't do it well enough'.

I consider spheres of responsibility as being like a balloon. Initially, it is empty but as you blow air into it, the balloon expands. As it continues to grow (due to increasing input), the surface tension becomes greater and the internal pressure mounts. If the amount being blown into the balloon is not regulated or stopped at a particular point, the tension and pressure will become too great and the inevitable (undesirable) outcome will occur — *pop*. To achieve the best result from your balloon-inflating duties, it can help to know when the balloon is becoming too pressurized and what the signs of impending disaster look and feel like. This will allow you to only put in the amount of air that the balloon can handle, or to let out some of the pressure that is causing the expansion.

So, if your sphere of responsibility becomes too big, you will experience increasing pressures and demands plus the tension of a system stretched beyond its capabilities. To reduce the impact and lessen another contributor to burnout, it is important to know your limits, to speak up and say that anything extra will create problems for you and your current workload. It can be helpful to release the tension by letting out some of that internal pressure — for example, by handing back some tasks or appropriately delegating them to colleagues. This is akin to releasing the air from the balloon in a controlled manner. Also, learn to be okay with asking questions about the extra work being given to you. One of the challenges in a demanding environment is that you may not feel confident in having conversations about whether the task or the associated timeframe is appropriate for you and the resources you have available.

A final point to notice is that sometimes we load ourselves up due to reasons such as wanting to help out, feeling that this fits our job description, or we are poor with boundaries. The latter leads to you perceiving that the task should be yours, when this may not actually be the case. By volunteering or taking on someone else's role, you add to your burden and relieve someone else of theirs. Altruistic maybe; self-destructive definitely.

6.

THE HARSH INTERNAL CRITIC: AN UNHELPFUL PASSENGER

People who value achievement do not want to be that person who 'failed' or underperformed. Such behaviour goes against the grain and highlights all the attributes that do not fit with expectations of the self. Due to this, the person might struggle to get past the behaviours or events that were not up to standard and were an embarrassment (to the self).

There tends to be difficulty in forgiving the self for these (sometimes perceived) errors or underperformance. This is often attached to a strong sense of self-criticism, which has already been noted as part of the internal make-up of many all-or-nothing people and some of those experiencing burnout. The tendency to psychologically beat yourself up comes about because such people want (nay, demand) more from themselves. Also, there continues to be misunderstanding and stigma around experiencing burnout. This can see people identifying themselves as failures or as being not good enough if they encounter burnout in their employment.

WHY DO I BEAT MYSELF UP?

It is hard for most of us to not be affected by comments from someone we trust, respect or rely upon. So, how much more powerful might it be if the message and the voice is a familiar one that we have lived with for a long time? Surely, if I am angry with myself or disappointed in myself it must be true, and for good reason? However, it is important to see that a central issue is usually overlooked by the overly focused individual: that these messages are not tangible. Indeed, they are thoughts — nothing else. The problem is the degree of emotional involvement with these thoughts, as well as the meaning and veracity we attribute to them. If we believe and assume that we are our thoughts and that they are true, then there is no room to manoeuvre — we become what we think and are then driven by these thoughts.

A word that keeps popping up through this exploration is 'believe', as in what we believe to be true. Unfortunately, the more we connect with our internal comments, the bigger the impact they can have, as we increasingly come to believe them. When you stop to think about it, language is simply a vehicle to convey ideas — powerful, for sure, but nevertheless the words aren't actually alive. It is the meaning we attach to them and the way we bond with them that can be the problem. This personal meaning tends to be associated with the 'not-quite-up-to-it' message for those who value achievement, one that is well rehearsed and may be very familiar to the readers of this book. If you have a 'need' to achieve, your manner might include demanding self-talk or rigidly expecting certain standards of yourself. The tone of this self-talk — this internal critic — can be clinical and distant and even harsh, without you necessarily realizing it. By remaining in a place where there are strong emotions, it proves difficult to shift away from the negativity and, often, a degree of 'stuckness' ensues along with an associated negative rehashing of events. Part of the difficulty here is that you probably don't fully understand why you are so angry at yourself. Nor do you consider that it is possible to change this. Perhaps the biggest issue for individuals in this situation is that they lose all sense of distance and objectivity about this ever-present but unhelpful passenger, this harsh inner critic. In essence, you become one with the language, fused with the thoughts and ideas expressed by this voice.

It can be hard, as a psychologist, to watch clients bullying themselves through their own internal talk. The effect this negative and judgmental self-evaluation has can be devastating for the person. It strips them of their confidence and, often, sees them unable to maintain a healthy sense of self.

Keisha is a young woman who presented with increasingly overwhelming feelings of anxiety and a sense that she was not a good enough friend, family member or employee. This was based on the self-identified observation that she did not help others enough and 'never' seemed to be able to 'be there' for people. She found it very difficult to be comfortable with her actions towards people she knew or came into contact with.

After any interaction, Keisha would play over and over again the things she'd said or what she could have done better. The language used to describe her behaviours was harsh, unrelenting and, quite simply, punitive. However, Keisha did not see it this way; she felt that she was justifiably calling herself to account and that the descriptors she employed for herself were appropriate. She described feeling that giving herself a psychological shake-up was a necessary step towards becoming a better friend or more caring person. From what I could tell, this self-denigration included the type of language and appraisals that Keisha would never, ever use towards another person. Yet, she lived this on a daily basis. As a result, Keisha struggled to feel good about any aspect of who she was and her self-confidence had been completely stripped away.

The main reason people tend to automatically run with these internal comments is because they come from the most trusted source: yourself. But what if you are not really the person being painted in these negative and unhelpful ways within your own mind? Surely, there is a chance that there is more to you than what is being portrayed in that instant, and in the language contained during that moment. Unfortunately, of course, each of these 'instances' is repeated over time and across a number of experiences, because you carry this harsh internal critic with you wherever you go and whatever you do. Perhaps it is time to pause and try to understand what this self-criticism is all about and why the harsh internal critic continues to come along for the journey?

For most A/N people and highly driven individuals, this self-criticism began in an early environment that promoted and expected high performance. Learning and understanding what is important and valued (by others) may have been intimately associated with negative feedback when goals were not achieved. On those occasions, any failure may have triggered a sense of personal embarrassment. The internal critic usually comes into being as a way of pushing the self to overcome poor performance and then (hopefully) go on to achieve as expected. The need to push oneself is bound in with this, as it seems a way to avoid 'failure' and hopefully experience some positive feedback. There would have been your own context in and around this self-critical behaviour from the start. There would also have been a reason for it developing, but this understanding might have become lost in the mists of time or so embedded in certain environments that the original reason is no longer considered. An exploration of this can lead to a more helpful consideration: perhaps, just perhaps, it is okay to be nicer to yourself. What if this is actually a potential, and one that might pay big dividends in the medium to long term?

If you think about it, over the years there will have been a lot of energy (emotional, cognitive and physical) expended in keeping this anger and disappointment around so you could put the person at fault (you) in their place. If this is the case, it might now be time to ask whether the original function is still valid. Additionally, it might be time to review what has been, up to now, accepted as an obvious and self-evident truth.

THE IMPACT OF SELF-CRITICISM

It is probable that self-criticism has the same internal effect as comments and judgments from other people. These self-generated comments may well trigger feelings of anxiety, anger or embarrassment — as if we were being verbally attacked by another person. Whichever direction this criticism comes from (internally or externally), it has essentially the same impact. The result is that you focus your attention inwardly and this leads to an evaluation of behaviour in a manner consistent with the tone of the comments: negatively. This means that we often internally shame ourselves through this harsh appraisal. In essence, there is a degree of threat involved here — not necessarily to life and limb, but to the sense of self and our personal identity.

Humans have developed powerful brains with the capacity to identify and perceive not only real, present threat but also *potential, future threat*. We are able to think and imagine, which provides us with the ability to conjure future problems and therefore feel angry, frightened or overwhelmed in response to an imagined situation. This same process is also possible in relation to internal threats, such as self-criticism. Although this is 'me' talking to and about 'myself', the older parts of the brain just know this is ugly and unpleasant. The brain therefore begins to respond in the same manner as if an external party, such as your boss, is making these negative comments. Threats are met with responses that can include significant arousal (physiological and emotional) and may set in motion strong behaviours and a readiness to respond to the threat.

Embarrassment and shame

To get to a place of high achievement in your chosen career, it is likely you have pushed yourself but possibly you've also been fearful of failing. Often attached to this driven approach is a degree of internal embarrassment or shame that is experienced as a result of encountering underperformance. But importantly, similar to the previous discussion on threat, we can also experience personal embarrassment from *potential* poor performances.

It can be helpful to realize there are various 'types' of personal embarrassment and shame, and this needs a bit of explanation. Here, these words relate to the negative internal views of yourself and your performance, but there can also be an externally directed sense of embarrassment. This relates to fearful beliefs around what others might think of you following your performance on a task. It is likely that the long-standing trait of self-criticism makes a person vulnerable to feeling embarrassment about themselves and their performance. You don't necessarily need to 'hate' yourself to feel internalized embarrassment. However, if there is an underlying hint of inadequacy this can be triggered. This is especially so if you are operating within a competitive environment such as a bonus system, or if promotion is being sought.

Strong emotional states such as personal embarrassment can feel very uncomfortable for most of us, and one way to deal with them is to avoid them if possible. A denial process or avoidance behaviours can work to keep the sense of self intact and safe — that is, you do something to ensure you won't encounter the unwanted feelings. You might find that you unwittingly throw yourself into the preparation process for meetings and projects at work to such an extent that the focus is on the doing rather than the feeling. The stronger the negative experience of emotions, the stronger the drive to avoid encountering or experiencing them may be. So, for example, you work very hard, for long hours. This behavioural response can be put in place via the classic demanding language that some high achievers tend to be guided by and use. Key words and phrases you might recognize and relate to from your internal dialogue include 'must', 'should', 'have to'. These have the effect of setting up an imperative situation, one where the listener (you) feels there is no choice or option. Unfortunately, avoidance behaviour will only act as a temporary buffer to the feelings bubbling away beneath the ever-present striving for goals.

It can be helpful for you to understand that the self-criticism and sense of embarrassment has come from somewhere and, perhaps more importantly, that it did a job. If we adopt more of a 'functional' approach to this, it can help us to feel okay about targeting the unhelpful self-criticism for what it is: a behaviour, and one that we adopted for a reason at some stage. Embarrassment is a reaction, but for our purposes it can also be seen as a driving force within the individual. It is usually in relation to something we feel uncomfortable about. Perhaps a key issue is how this expresses itself when you encounter difficulties or 'failure'. People who drive themselves to achieve may feel the need to prove to themselves and others that they are capable. If the sense of self is built solely upon achievement, then the individual can become exquisitely sensitive to, and primed for action in relation to, particular threats — in this case, potential failure. This priming may mean that the threshold the person responds to (the point at which they feel threatened) is lowered and therefore the threat is, in effect, experienced as greater than it might actually be. Such a situation can result in the harsh internal critic being triggered more easily and, over time, more frequently. This can then result in increased levels of self-criticism and a heightened sense of inadequacy. When these are put alongside the goal of high achievement, the combination can bring about a sense of personal embarrassment due to what is perceived as underperformance.

TURNING DOWN THE VOLUME

Each of us needs to find a way to step back from these negative ideas, thoughts and internal comments. By doing this, you can better develop a degree of objectivity, which can help keep you safe from the potentially harmful and destabilizing effects of such comments. To lessen or take away the negative effects of this self-criticism, you will benefit from replacing this unhelpful dialogue with something more helpful, or at least less undermining.

The fact that strong emotions are involved mean it is not as simple as 'telling myself things will be better and there isn't really a problem'. Even if you have developed some awareness, it might not be easy to bring about change by just saying, 'I won't do this again'. Self-blaming needs to be replaced with something else, something that accommodates heightened (and raw) emotions such as personal embarrassment. Tolerating the distress and concern around feeling inadequate (remember: this may well be a biased perception and not a reality) is also important. It is more helpful in the long run if you can move on from avoidance of these feelings. A new goal could be to work with your internal dialogue, plus start to be somewhat kinder to yourself. If you can see the negativity within a context, then you can start to see that there is some choice about whether you treat yourself in such a manner.

As with all things in life, there is usually a reason for our behaviour; it serves some sort of purpose. For the overachiever, this behaviour is often associated with fear of failure, such as not living up to their own exacting standards. By focusing solely upon the task and outcome, you unfortunately tend to overlook the process and don't take note of how important your efforts and experiences are. Some individuals expect a lot of themselves and tend not to give due credit for the effort put in — they only see that they have fallen short of the mark. Nor have they learned to value effort for its own sake. You might be overlooking the fact that there is a process, or journey, involved and that this might be equally as important to the outcome.

Interestingly, when a therapist introduces the idea of a client learning to cut themselves some slack, the hardworking individual often recoils in horror. This is usually accompanied by an immediate sense that such an approach would not be appropriate or even possible. Sitting behind this is a long learning history of seeing anything other than full-on effort as being slack, self-indulgent or perhaps the biggest insult of all: lazy. It can be quite sad to witness this struggle within clients to care for themselves or see the merit in judging themselves by the kinder standards they apply to others. When you ask these people how they relate to others who struggle, they can invariably come up with appropriate explanations and reasons for why those people might not have met their goals. The driven individual can demonstrate an ability to account for context and the intangible factors that can impact performance — but usually only for others. If you can relate to this, you probably also find it very difficult to account for such variables and how they relate to yourself. As if different rules within the universe apply to you! This is so unfair, as it means mistakes are constantly replayed and the resulting sense of anger, personal embarrassment and heartache colours the ability to feel good about yourself.

Constant self-judging has become an art form for most high achieving and A/N people. Although it might have started long ago and for possibly understandable reasons, this function has now become lost in the passage of time. Individuals seem able to hold onto an awareness that they learned to shape their performance around how to do things 'correctly'. Similarly, they can often see that this learning was related to getting better and then maintaining the new high(er) standards. However, over time, it has gone beyond this positive guidance phase and become more like the classic Sergeant Major who yells, demands and harasses to get immediate and uniform responses.

It is important to acknowledge that high achievers are not continuously engaged in an internal battle where they scream at themselves inside their own heads, day and night. Rather, this self-bullying (for that is what it really has become) tends to be triggered when they encounter challenges and poor performance. It is also important to note that this behaviour doesn't necessarily signal a strong sense of hatred towards the self. The majority of high achieving or burnt-out people I have met are not caught up in an overwhelming sense of personal dislike. Rather, they have come to believe this criticism is part of learning to meet goals and excel; interesting indeed, that they have chosen a benign and helpful interpretation of such a negative behaviour. Unfortunately, this criticism has got out of control and become so automatic that they may not recognize when they are doing it, let alone to what extent. Given that most people basically like themselves and are comfortable spending time with themselves, it should be possible to help people learn to disengage from this unhelpful approach.

Learning to disengage

You will be pleased to hear that the goal of shifting this behaviour is not to turn yourself into an 'average' or 'lazy' person. Rather, it is about helping you to apply the same realistic standards that you might regularly apply to others. A key factor is helping you to be able to disengage from the harsh internal critic at important times, such as when you are starting to struggle or are encountering a setback. It is about helping you to also see that this negative self-talk taps into strong emotions; it is not just about words inside the head. These words relate to, trigger and may also enhance emotions. The words and emotions are also related to memories and contexts. This is how the brain operates; it likes to group things together as this is an efficient sorting and retrieval system. I often tell clients that the 'flavour' of a thought is transmitted and opens up other parts of the network, but generally only those aspects with the same 'flavour'. So, if our responses to a challenge or setback are negative and self-deprecatory, then the thoughts and emotions around this are more likely to be unhelpful as well. These will access the memory banks and open up folders of similar unsuccessful encounters or outcomes. Obviously, this is less than helpful if you are trying to work through a difficult situation and all you can recall are previous 'failures'.

It is important to realize that you can't eliminate these emotions by throwing yourself into more of the behaviour, such as pushing on with the task no matter what. Being angry at the self will not bring about the goal of being perfect; the latter is not actually possible, anyway. Flexibility needs to be tapped into, so that the standards applied are beneficial and realistic (and no, that does not mean second-rate!). Simply beating yourself up psychologically does not solve anything.

It can also help to learn to pull back and get some perspective, to see if you are applying (to yourself) the same rules you apply to the rest of the world. The sense of personal embarrassment mentioned earlier is triggered because the person who is desperate to achieve does not want to see themselves as that person who has 'failed'. What if this 'black and white' application of rules and judgment could be shifted so that you realize you might not have failed, therefore you do not need to feel this sense of embarrassment?

In essence, self-critical judging has brought about a conflict with the primary value of being on top of things and being able to 'cope'. It can help to learn that a better approach is to adjust expectations, rather than simply starting to be 'nice' to yourself, which can bring up images of self-indulgence. This is about being brave enough to look at things differently and not to just go with the well-rehearsed comments from long ago. Adjusting expectations is *not* about giving up on standards. If anything, it is a refinement of a balance between achievement and sustainability. From such a perspective, a more solid sense of self may begin to emerge, one that can cope with achievements, challenges *and* disappointments. Now, doesn't that sound like a better recipe for (sustainable) success?

TO SUM UP

There is a voice that you know well and it is not always a comforting or even supportive one. This familiarity makes it hard to ignore, and also gives the statements an air of authenticity — or is that authority? As a result, you have probably come to accept the comments as appropriate and 'true'. However, you are hopefully now beginning to realize that this harsh internal critic is not really concerned with motivating you or even helping you to up your game and be more successful. Rather, it is a long-standing expression of the negativity and fear related to performance and achievement. The language employed is more about pointing out your perceived shortcomings than offering active problem-solving approaches. Why this voice is hard to ignore is simple: it is your own!

Messages that have been given to us by important others are powerful and, if they are said often enough, we take them onboard. This results in us using them as guidelines, and they help shape our expectations of ourselves. What we tend to forget is that these messages were from a particular context but they now have a life of their own and seem to relate to *all* aspects of our lives. Perhaps it is time to pause and ask whether the original context is still relevant or indeed valid anymore? Maybe by doing this you can start to explore other ways of making sense of your performance and identify new ways that not only help you solve problems but also motivate you.

Because this unhelpful passenger so eagerly points out where we go wrong, we seem to either be constantly near a crisis of confidence or repeatedly confronted with our perceived inabilities. This has implications for how we see ourselves and can result in a sense of personal embarrassment. This is a problem, as we may then struggle to let go of the 'failures', run the risk of being overwhelmed by strong negative emotions and might also find it difficult to ask for help. This chews up a lot of emotional energy and can get us stuck in a rut, whereby it is hard to generate any positivity about ourselves or our potential.

There is room in our lives for appropriate, objective and realistic self-appraisal, as these things can help us to finetune our performance, adjust and adapt. However, the harsh internal critic is neither objective nor realistic much of the time. As a result, you might be unfairly judging your performance and becoming acutely aware of what you have done 'wrong' — yet not notice all the things you did right. It is only fair that you offer yourself the chance to see if you are being realistic and, if not, it might be time to dampen the authority that seems to come along with this critical voice.

A chance for change

No, having a voice inside your head telling you how badly you are doing is not a sign of madness. This familiar voice — which excels in pointing out your mistakes — isn't an alien intruder. It is a looped recording of long-standing messages about perfect performance and pushing yourself that is expressed in your own 'speak'. It often represents the lessons given to you by others long ago, about always being the best.

A key approach to dealing with this unwanted and unhelpful passenger is to find ways to dampen the volume, decrease the impact and lessen the hold the messages have upon you. In fact, what would be really beneficial is if you can reframe the familiar role of this voice from that of a 'harsh internal critic' to one of a 'quality control advisor'. This makes it possible to hear the messages from a different perspective and see the 'feedback' (*not criticism*) as an opportunity to monitor your progress and adjust as needed.

A helpful approach is to learn to refocus your perspective from the critical approach to a more positive one that affirms you. The challenge is to gain a more balanced view of events and adopt a more supportive stance with yourself. Within this, try to identify what your strengths and skills are, rather than just seeing that things have come unstuck. Remind yourself of previous times when you have been able to fix things, use appropriate strategies or problem-solve issues. These may well reflect a more accurate image of your ability. By tapping into previous achievements and good outcomes, you will disengage from the parts of your brain associated with responding to threat. Those areas are the ones that kick your nervous system into overdrive and ready you for any threat. Unfortunately, if you are in a negative or defeatist frame of mind, this will only key you into your perceived failures more and more. Conversely, if you can generate a more positive and accepting stance to your situation, you have a better chance of activating those parts of the brain related to feeling good and being in control. Surely this is a better place from which to explore problem-solving options?

If you have got this far through the book, it is time to consider not slavishly following the unhelpful thoughts and expectations you have, at times, about yourself and your abilities. For example, when confronted with a difficult situation do you see the world from a singular perspective, one that might trap you into potentially unfair conclusions about your abilities? If you challenge those critical messages, you may be able to avoid the self-defeating behaviours that often come racing in next.

An effective way to begin doing this is to attend to what happens when you encounter a difficult situation. You might notice that you immediately have thoughts telling you how useless you are or that the task is beyond you. Up until now, these automatic and negative thoughts might have been accepted as being gospel. But what is the actual evidence for these statements? How true are they and is there another perspective? Simple questions like these fit with the way the brain operates and they are much better than just yelling at yourself! The brain is a logical machine, and if you set it a question, you engage the logic circuitry rather than the negative, self-bashing, emotional mechanisms. Such questions also allow you to see if the harsh statements are actually true. If they don't stand up to logical scrutiny, you may be able to replace these unhelpful thoughts and comments with more useful alternatives.

TRY THIS

Have a piece of paper and a pen handy. Recall a recent time when a task at work wasn't going too well. Once you get a clear memory or image of the event, try to focus on the thoughts that came into your mind about things not working out. They may have been something like 'Here we go again, another stuff up' or 'Useless sod, you can't get anything right' or even 'This is hopeless, what's the point?'. Of course, there are many variations on this theme but for a lot of driven people, the automatic thoughts they have in response to difficulties are self-blaming and negative.

Next, write down a very brief description of the situation and then beside this what the immediate thoughts were. Now repeat this same process three more times with different situations. Note: the situations you choose don't have to be major catastrophes.

Do you notice anything about the type of thoughts and words that were running through your head at these challenging times? Did they set you up to feel good about yourself and help with problem solving or …?

Now for each thought you have written down, ask yourself at least two of the following simple questions:
- What is the actual evidence for these statements?
- How true are these comments or beliefs?
- Is there another perspective I could take?

What does the logical, non-emotional part of your brain offer as answers to these new questions? Might the answers set you on a different course than the previously accepted, negative comments? If so, perhaps you could give this simple technique a go — challenging your thoughts with the above questions — next time you encounter a challenging situation.

TRY THIS

Another useful technique to deal with the harsh internal critic and its comments is to shift to an external or different perspective. To do this, ask yourself what a valued and trusted friend, colleague or mentor might say in response to the situation you are encountering. This requires a bit of pre-planning but, once sorted, it can be a powerful way to help yourself disengage from the internal bashing you are receiving or are about to receive. To use this technique, think of someone you know well and whose opinion you trust implicitly. Try to choose a person who has qualities that are opposite to the harsh, demeaning approach of the internal critic. Think of someone who is level-headed, able to sort out reality from a fearful appraisal and perhaps is also able to generate options for managing difficult situations. These are the types of attributes you could benefit from encountering in place of the current unhelpful and self-deprecating statements. It is hard to simply 'replace' longstanding ways of seeing the world, so this technique helps you try new ones on for size and become familiar with them.

Let's now put this approach into practice. Recall a situation (social or work related) where things were going wrong and you were being critical of yourself. Settle back in a quiet, comfortable environment and try to recall the putdowns that were offered up to yourself about this event. Not nice, were they?! What is the effect on you of hearing these words and interpretations of the events? Write these down, so you can see them in all their gory detail.

Now, see if you can visualize the person whose opinion or perspective you trust and try to hear their voice. The aim is to hear what this person might say about the difficulties encountered or the mistakes made. If you know this person well, you will have a fair idea of what they will say, plus how they will interpret the situation and outcomes. Allow yourself to listen to this person and consider their take on the situation. How is it different to what you were saying to yourself, and what is the effect of hearing this different perspective? Remember, this new 'voice' or perspective is from someone you trust and therefore it is worthwhile acknowledging that their take may well be valid and one that you could consider adopting.

Practise the above approach by reviewing past situations — first from your own perspective and then from that of the trusted advisor. If you can make the image of this person as real as possible and hear their voice, you will be better able to relate to their message. When you are next in a challenging situation and you notice that you are starting to dump on yourself, pause, take a few calming breaths and then ask yourself: What would [make sure you name them] say about this or about my performance? Hopefully, this will allow you to consider an alternative perspective and, after a while, you might find that you don't automatically criticize yourself and your efforts.

7.
STRIVING FOR PERFECTION, OR NEEDING TO BE PERFECT?

In my clinic, I have noticed that perfectionism is often part of the lived experience of people who have burnout. In this chapter, we will consider the strong attention to detail and high expectations that some overwhelmed and over-pressurized people operate by. They regularly strive to do their best but tend to be bitterly disappointed if the result is not top notch.

In some people there can be a powerful drive that can see them become overly focused on a task until they reach a (very) high, self-set level of accomplishment. The fear of not producing a perfect performance may even lead to a type of cognitive paralysis or procrastination. This is where the driven individual may not be willing to start a project due to a sense that it will not be up to the level they require. High levels of conscientiousness have long been associated with the development of burnout, and underperforming (or feeling as though goals can't/won't be met) grates with this aspect of the personality. There is a connection between an internal perfection driver and these higher levels of conscientiousness. As a result, this chapter will explore how perfectionistic tendencies fit in with, or even promote, burnout in some people.

It is important for us to acknowledge and account for the reality that we take our personalities to work and bring them home again. This can see our high standards and expectations flow towards work and then back home with us afterwards. We also know that the experience of burnout does not stay attached to the workplace. One point I would like to add to this understanding is that, when we are feeling overwhelmed, unsure and don't seem to be coping, we often retreat to the comfort of what feels natural and usual. As a result, you might find yourself automatically relying on your well-rehearsed behaviours to get through the challenges of each day. For the purposes of our current conversation, this can mean that — even if you are on leave from work — you may find yourself becoming grumpy and upset at the 'chaos', 'mess' and lack of 'effort' from family members. Their behaviours might seem designed to frustrate and upset you, while placing more demands on you to clean up after them. However, it may actually be that nothing is different at home or with the family. It could be that you are desperately (and unwittingly) seeking control in your uncertain world by focusing more on having things 'right' and 'correct'. This will be an annoyance for you but an absolute pain for your family.

As the title of this chapter suggests, there are certain traits that can have an important influence on how we approach things. Particularly relevant is the issue of perfectionistic traits. It is not being suggested that these are fully formed at birth, nor do they appear complete at a particular birthday or milestone. Rather, these traits are developed over time and can also be shaped by forces external to the individual. Within all of us, there may be more or less of a natural tendency to focus on things being 'right'. (For our purposes, though, we are not considering clinical conditions such as obsessive compulsive disorder or autism spectrum disorders, both of which can have a strong focus on orderliness, correctness and specificity.) However, some people exhibit strong traits that promote a need to have things completed, usually accompanied by an emphasis on correctness and high quality. Therefore, to make more sense of this style of interacting with the world, it can be helpful to gain a grasp of factors relevant to perfection. Perhaps by understanding this a bit better, you will see that perfectionism is not a matter of being completely present or not; neither is it entirely useful or entirely problematic. The truth is that you can lean towards high standards and doing a great job but also have some flexibility to tolerate the occasional not-so-great performance. If you can view perfectionistic traits (and expressions of these) as being on a continuum, then you will not need to eliminate the desire to do well. A better understanding of this internal pressure and learning to identify when it is starting to impact events will allow you to more evenly apply its expression.

TRUE CONFESSION TIME

As a group, clinical psychologists tend to skew towards being perfectionists. The question is whether the training makes one like this or whether people like this are attracted to the profession. I think it is the latter. We tend to find it difficult to write short reports as we might leave something 'important' out. Additionally, we tend to angst over the 'right' words to ensure the accuracy of what we are trying to say.

I have to put my hand up to say that I have leant towards perfectionistic tendencies for many years. My excuse is that I was born a Virgo, a star sign that inherently describes perfection and fussiness (now there's an example of a rationalization if ever I saw one!). My wife has been raising an eyebrow for many a year at my perseverance with tasks beyond what is actually necessary. A good example of this is within my chosen hobby of restoring old Japanese motorcycles. One might say this has become an outlet for my perfectionistic tendencies, as I have endeavoured to restore my bikes to the exact specifications they had when they left the factory in Japan over 50 years ago. In the spirit of openness, I shall share an example that illustrates my sameness-as-you and also underlines the problems (and, sometimes, pointlessness) of perfectionistic tendencies.

I needed to replace the brake linings on my 1971 Kawasaki 500 and immediately set out on an international quest to find original brake shoes, with the factory-original linings. This was due to my belief that for the bike to be correct, it had to be 100 per cent correct — that is, all parts had to be the same as the day it left Japan. I eventually found a set on eBay and entered a bidding war with some gentleman in Estonia, who obviously thought the same as me. The cost went up and up (in US dollars) but I was determined to win and eventually did so. The price of postage was not insignificant either, *but* I did have the original shoes and linings. This, of course, meant my restoration was going to be 'correct'.

After fitting the new shoes and test-riding the bike, I was disappointed with the braking performance and also frustrated that my efforts were no advance on the problem I was addressing. I expressed this to a fellow rider who has much more mechanical nous than me, and he brusquely stated, 'What the heck did you expect?' and then added, 'You bought a 50-year-old product which is made of obsolete and inefficient material and expected it to perform well in the 21st century.' After more discussion, he went on to add that I could have taken the old shoes into a local brake centre and had the linings redone with a modern compound that would have been much more effective and cost me a fraction of what I paid. He also pointed out the (now) blindingly obvious fact that no one can actually see what material the linings are made of, as they are hidden inside the wheel!

Hmmm, food for thought ... and personal reflection, perhaps. What this episode taught me was that the quest to obtain perfection can lead to a single-minded following of a pathway even though there might be more realistic, practical (and cheaper) options that could achieve the same or better outcome. By obtaining an outside perspective, I was now able to see that I could attain the goals I had set myself plus enjoy the outcomes for what they were, rather than what I felt they should have been. In reality, even with modern brake linings the bike will look original.

DEFINING PERFECTIONISM

There is currently no complete or universally agreed-upon definition of perfectionism. However, there is some acceptance that it may consist of a number of aspects. This can include it being a characteristic of personality but also that it involves some aspects of cognition (thoughts and processing) plus behaviour. There also seems to be some agreement amongst researchers and therapists that it involves the setting of high standards and may, for some, be accompanied by self-criticism when personal standards are not met. Sounding familiar to you?

However, striving to be the best you possibly can be is not necessarily a bad thing, and it is a well-evidenced truth that setting high standards can have a lot of positive spin-offs. Where would the Olympic Games be if standards were not set at a high level? They would, in effect, be a pretty mediocre track meet with any country bumpkin able to turn up and throw a spear about. Instead, we see the positive pursuit of high standards, celebration of success and the many positive aspects of a global interaction. As you will hopefully come to see, having high goals and standards is not the problem — but nor does this have to be a major character flaw.

PROBLEMS ACCOMPANYING THE QUEST FOR PERFECTION

If we are to better understand perfectionism and therefore its impact on the person with burnout, we need to realize that it is about much more than just the setting of high standards. There can also be concern about mistakes or poor performance and some doubt about personal potential. Additionally, many perfectionists struggle with the ability to congratulate themselves and be comfortable with *any* level of achievement. It is suggested here that these aspects are, to some degree, present in and relevant to people with burnout and those with A/N personality types.

Such people tend to judge their performance, at any given point, not only by high standards but also the critical self-evaluation discussed in the previous chapter. If performance can be evaluated without slipping into this negative self-judgment, it should be possible to modulate one of the unhealthy drivers that maintains the singular focus on outcomes. It may well be that the negative self-evaluation is acting as a pathway away from realistic, positive goal-setting and leading instead to the less helpful driving of oneself to get the perfect outcome. Thus, to make better sense of what drives you and to better understand the impact of your behaviours, bear in mind this negative, regularly running commentary. The unhelpful passenger may be one of the important aspects of what turns high standards from the positive and useful to the maladaptive.

The high standards of a perfectionist can also be directed towards other people, where the perfectionist comes to expect or demand that others perform to a similarly high standard. However, this can be patently unfair at times. The other person may have no idea they are being judged or held to account, which can make it bewildering (and frustrating) that they are thought of as 'not up to it' by the person evaluating them. This of course is a potential recipe for disaster and strife in both personal and professional situations. The perfectionist can, at times, become so disenchanted by others (who don't even know they are under scrutiny) that they begin to express their frustration. This may be to the point where they consider it impossible to 'trust' others to do the right thing. One outcome is that they do not delegate tasks, plus they may have a sense of disappointment and disillusionment about those they work with. This can then lead to the perfectionist adding to their own workload — with an imbalance in the dynamics and operating levels with co-workers or employees. Obviously, this adds to the burden of tasks and can see the individual push themselves to do even more. This is in the mistaken belief that others are not up to the task and the only person they can rely on is ... themselves. Over time, this builds up the workload and increases the risk of burnout.

A final twist in this tale is that perfectionists often believe the high levels of achievement they exhibit are demanded and expected of them by others. They see this as an inescapable trap, as they are convinced others are holding them to very high standards. Unfortunately, many people who have experienced burnout do not regularly pause to check out whether, indeed, these expectations are true. If you talk to workers who operate like this (particularly if they are returning after time off work) you will find that they often push beyond their tolerance levels. Essentially, they are responding to a combination of their own internal demands and the perceived expectations from their colleagues, manager or employer. Interestingly, when you encourage these individuals to actually ask the employer about their performance and to establish what the expectations are, there is often clear feedback that the boss is happy with the output. Unfortunately, at times, much of the pressure and performance concerns can be self-generated.

As stated earlier, having high standards is not necessarily all bad. However, when these standards are aligned with a rigid style of thinking, the result can be a merciless striving for unrealistic goals, with internal chastising that acts as a negative energizer. I recall a client whose passion was pigeon breeding and racing. He identified potential benefits from having the best possible environment for his birds to live in. As a result, he set about building them a new aviary. This was going to be the Taj Mahal of aviaries and something that would also bring him kudos amongst fellow fanciers. However, it never quite got finished as there were always adjustments and modifications that 'needed' to be done. Don't you just love that qualifying word? When I reflected that he had been working on this project for nigh on seven years (!) he offered multiple reasons why things weren't up to the required standard. The question then became, just who was he doing this for and whose standards was he trying to meet? As far as I could tell (and I readily admit to being no expert on pigeons), his birds had been eating, preening, sleeping, doing the stuff that pigeons do and happily making baby pigeons within the old, apparently unsatisfactory, housing over this entire seven-year period. In contrast, the breeder was a frustrated and unhappy man who could only see that things were 'not quite right yet'.

When goals slip from your grasp, the self-criticism becomes stronger and you can experience a double whammy of personal embarrassment and guilt related to the perceived 'failure'. This is a sense of shame that you have not lived up to your own standards and those you believe others are holding you to. The guilt is around having let yourself down, plus the concern that you have shown the world you were not up to the task. I do not believe for a second that it is wrong to aim for high levels of achievement. However, what if you build your sense of self around this issue, such that it rests solely upon the attainment? Such a situation has the potential to turn things towards the negative and problematic. The issue is that if you start to see yourself as being capable or worthwhile *only* when you achieve highly, you cannot consider yourself capable or worthwhile if you do a less-than-perfect job. The problem for some people is that they tend to apply their high standards to everything attempted in the important areas of their life — then judge themselves solely by outcomes rather than effort. Unfortunately, if one area is perceived as deficient, this can be enough to wipe away all other achievements no matter how many other projects were actually successful. This is partly why burnout has such far-reaching implications for your enjoyment and feelings of worth in your wider family, and in the social and recreational dimensions of life. In essence, you could end up discounting your successes and placing an emphasis upon your failures (i.e. what went wrong at work). Over time, this opens the door for a level of negative self-judgment that can have implications for mood levels and personal confidence. At this point, I ask you to pause and consider if any of this is resonating with you as the reader (and possibly someone who has experienced burnout).

THE GOOD, THE BAD AND THE UGLY (OUTCOMES)

Clinical understanding of perfection shows it to be both complex and multilevel. Research suggests there can be both positive and negative dimensions of perfection. Additionally, it is clear that some people can live with and manage this drive for top performance and excellent outcomes. Ellam-Dyson and Palmer refer to 'healthy perfectionists' who are able to focus on and work towards a desired goal but *do not* have the tendency to give themselves a hard time if they do not meet their aims. These 'healthy perfectionists' therefore do not seem to embody a key (negative) element we have looked at — the harsh internal critic.

This raises an interesting point: what if contributing factors to burnout are strong perfectionistic traits plus the internal critic? If so, might it be possible to bring about a more positive approach by learning to manage that critic and develop a 'healthy' approach to perfectionism? This may bring about a more manageable, yet positive, focus and begin to dial down the tendency to push too far and hard. It may also help bring about a change in how workplace tasks are approached without altering the essence of who you are (e.g. someone who wishes to do well in their career). What if you could keep valued aspects of yourself, such as being achievement-focused, while modulating the level of effort on tasks, and therefore reduce personal levels of angst and stress? For perfectionists operating at Ellam-Dyson and Palmer's 'unhealthy' end of the spectrum, the stress is prolonged and is a bit like driving your car with one foot on the brake while pressing the accelerator harder and harder, all the while expecting more performance. In the short term, little happens to the car except higher levels of unpleasant noise. However, if this inappropriate driving style continues, parts of the motor will begin to be affected. For you, as a person, this can mean physical, cognitive or emotional wear and tear!

Within clinical work and related literature, it has long been noted that rigidly operating with high standards can be risky. In recent times, more and more research reinforces this point. We now think that perfectionism has a role to play in the beginning and maintenance of a number of clinical problems. Some examples of these are anxiety-based conditions, mood problems and eating disorders. The type of perfectionism relevant here is the intrapersonal one, whereby high expectations are placed upon yourself to achieve goals that may actually be unrealistic or unsustainable. Unfortunately, there often is no self-limiting or adjusting mechanism inherent in this process. Thus, once you reach the goal, you immediately reset the target — but always in an upward direction. This is due to the fact that you feel the initial level must have been too easy if you were able to meet it! It therefore becomes increasingly harder to meet the self-set goals and you find yourself on a 'mission impossible'. As a result, you might become vulnerable to anxiety and/or depression.

If you engage with the world via a strongly operating perfection driver, you could be at higher risk of mood-related problems should things not go according to plan. Therefore, the perfectionistic approach to life might be a legitimate target if the aim is to bring about meaningful change. For those who have suffered burnout, focusing solely on either mood or anxiety may be akin to only smoothing the upper edges of the proverbial iceberg — there is much more lurking below the surface that can continue to create problems. However, if the perfectionistic tendencies can be modulated, gains may be achieved with the unhealthy style of behaviour, e.g. overdoing things *plus* any mood and anxiety issues that are impacting the individual.

You will have noticed by now that this book is not about eliminating or 'curing' problems. Rather, it presents an approach of understanding what factors are operating within you at a given time and then considering how to modulate these. To this end, empowering yourself with knowledge and skills about all aspects of the drive to be perfect will have a more lasting impact than just being told to lower your standards a bit. Remember that old adage about teaching a person how to fish rather than just giving them a fish to eat? It is a waste of therapeutic energy to simply suggest to you, the person with burnout, that your high standards need to be eliminated. This is threatening; as you know full well, such a perspective has helped you achieve highly. If it is suggested that you simply let go of this approach, you will feel vulnerable, and the tendency to all-or-nothing thinking will immediately take you to a place of fear that you will become a slob with no standards ... and therefore no potential!

There is a wealth of well-established therapeutic approaches with techniques to help you gain a sense of mastery over the perfection driver you might have been living with. Two of these approaches are Cognitive Behavioural Therapy (CBT) and Acceptance and Commitment Therapy (ACT). Both of these therapies posit that cognitions (thoughts, appraisals and decisions) plus their resulting behaviours can not only create problems but also keep alive the associated difficulties. The approach put forward by this book is to help you learn which 'driver' is being triggered, plus when the unhelpful thoughts, feelings and comments are coming into play. This is so that you can manage or modulate the symptoms.

When I first met Li, she had been off work for around three months. From her description, this time away had followed eighteen months of struggle, disenchantment and despair within her role as a team leader of twelve people. With a palpable feeling of sadness, Li outlined how she had been working extra hours and experiencing her (previously enjoyable) role as 'too much' and 'beyond me'. She also described how she had stopped going to the gym and found it challenging to spend time actively engaged with her two young children. Everything at home seemed to frustrate her and nothing her partner or children did was 'right'. After several sessions of exploring what might have brought Li to this unwanted situation, we were able to identify a number of strong schemas that she was operating by within the work environment. Prime amongst these was the need to have things completed to the highest possible standard, because she was responsible for the department's outcome and their contribution to the company's performance.

Li had always been focused on achieving the best possible outcome but, as things became busier at work, she found herself increasingly worried about attaining the standards she felt were necessary. As we unpacked her work engagement, it became clear that Li had taken on tasks that her team members would usually complete. She came to realize that this was due to a fear that her colleagues might not do things 'the right way' or to 'the standard that's expected'. The outcome was that Li spent her breaks doing or redoing these other tasks plus her own role. As the months went on, Li became worn down (physically and emotionally), until she felt there was no option other than taking extended sick leave.

Our work together focused on understanding the power of her perfection driver and its effect on Li's choices. We looked at how she might better detect when this schema was being triggered and how she might dial it down. A big gain for us came when we looked at how Li might be able to decline her internal demands to take things on. With her return to work, we looked at how she might delegate work and distribute tasks according to the skill sets of each of her team. This specifically addressed her fear that the employee might not be able to handle the tasks. This was a gradual process where Li learned to trust her decision-making and her colleagues. The overall outcome was a less demanding work schedule for Li, with fewer feelings of stress and inadequacy. She also noted that her team members were demonstrating greater levels of initiative and reported feeling increasingly positive about their roles — because they were able to challenge themselves and grow within their role. A win-win situation.

To make lasting behavioural change, it might not be useful to focus on altering the high standards in isolation. Rather, it will be of more benefit to learn how to manage the self-critical voice that comments on and promotes unhelpful behaviours. So if you are setting career goals, don't think that you have to aim low. Your perfectionistic streak can serve you well as you undertake projects within the workplace, as it has the potential to help you achieve highly and demonstrate your abilities. The key is to ensure that you are motivated by positive reinforcement and the pursuit of excellence, as opposed to being driven by a fear of failure or the quest for perfection. The latter is more likely to result in you focusing on possible errors plus putting in longer hours, with potentially less efficiency and reduced job satisfaction. The former should result in you setting clearer goals and, if it is complemented by a high sense of self-efficacy, you may be able to more confidently move in a beneficial direction.

TO SUM UP

Perfectionistic traits, or high standards, are not evil or wrong. However, they can sometimes take on a life of their own and become unhelpful. Indeed, they can become a trap that is hard to escape from, one where we begin to expect ourselves to be perfect. Ask yourself, in the cold light of day, whether perfection is actually a realistic or attainable goal. I can tell you now that it is not. Therefore, you may be setting yourself up for some heavy-duty heartache whereby you constantly feel that you are failing, only to then readjust your goals. Unfortunately, this tends to be upwards, rather than towards a realistic level. These perfectionistic traits are not, in and of themselves, a problem. Rather, it is what you do with them that counts.

If you strive to improve, you can go places that were previously inaccessible. Think about top athletes and their constant quest to run faster, throw further or jump higher. These high achievers readjust and realign their goals and technique to the nth degree, but they also realize that subtle changes can pay big dividends. Unfortunately, if the quest for better performance is accompanied by harsh judgment and negative criticism then things can come unstuck quite quickly. This is particularly so during times of stress, pressure and demand — when one needs to perform at one's peak.

There can be a 'healthy' perfection driver, where we challenge ourselves to extend our performance and try to go further in a desired direction for positive reasons. There is also the less positive perfection driver, where we dump on ourselves immediately and continuously when we do not meet the targets we set for ourselves. Unfortunately, many high achieving people tend to operate in the realm of the latter. As a result, when you encounter situations where you do not meet the self-set high goals, you tend to be confronted by a disparaging appraisal of the performance (sadly, your own). This way of approaching life comes with risks, such as lowered confidence, anxiety, a variable mood ... plus burnout.

You might find that your goals are being shaped by unhelpful and perhaps misperceived information. This is usually self-generated, but it can leak out so that you start to second-guess the expectations of others and whether they are judging you. Many hard-working people drive themselves to meet targets or levels of operating that they believe are being set by external people and agencies. Unfortunately, such people do not always take time to check in with these significant others to see if the expectations and standards are as they believe. What if you have been pushing yourself needlessly and bringing about unnecessary pressures and problems? While there are some workplaces where the external standards are even higher than one's own, the point here is to check things out first — rather than drive yourself to distraction based on assumptions.

All things in moderation is a good maxim. This applies to the goals and expectations you set yourself. With ever increasing standards comes a potentially disproportionate cost in terms of physical, cognitive and emotional energy. The extra effort put in to get an A+ on an exam is usually well beyond the actual, measurable difference between an A and an A+. This is not to suggest you shouldn't try to extend yourself or do better. You should, however, weigh things up within a personal and functional context and then make a conscious decision on the effort to be expended in relation to the value of the goal you are setting. This is instead of automatically driving yourself to achieve at a higher level without understanding what is behind such decisions. Don't throw away your desire to achieve or make gains. Instead, try to understand what is driving you at any point and check in to see if the goals are *realistic*, *attainable* and *appropriate*.

A chance for change

Language can trap us. Perhaps it is time to give some thought to how you verbally prepare for tasks and, more importantly, how you talk to yourself if things don't turn out perfectly. If, before you start a task, you regularly find yourself using phrases like 'I must ...', 'I have to ...' or 'This needs to be ...', then you could be following that perfection driver. Try replacing those demanding words and phrases with ones that give you a chance of succeeding, such as 'A realistic timeframe for this would be ...' or 'The options for this are ...'.

If, after the task is done, you find yourself using unhelpful, derogatory and judgmental phrases, you are probably stuck in that unpleasant space ruled by the harsh internal critic. Try focusing on what you did achieve, rather than what you didn't. If you are starting to judge your performance harshly, refer back to p. 99 and the discussion of using a trusted person as a guide or perspective giver. Then, ask yourself: 'What would [name of your trusted person] say about my performance today?' This way you are not generalizing about all performances and letting that automatic negative thinking kick into gear.

> **TRY THIS**
>
> Your perfection driver is probably embedded deeply in schemas that were laid down long ago. To lessen the impact, you might need a step-by-step strategy to 'de-automate' the process. *Before* you start a task or project, follow the steps below.
>
> 1. Ask yourself, 'What is my goal today, with this task, here, in front of me now?'
> 2. Reflect on your honest answer then ask yourself, 'Is it reasonable and fair to expect the performance, outcome or timeframe that I have just set myself?'
> 3. If the answer is no, then go back to Step 1 and recalibrate your answer to account for the realities of this situation *here and now* (not what your perfection driver is saying).
> 4. Move on to Step 2 again and ask yourself the same question. If the answer is still no, go back to Step 1 again. Repeat this process as often as it takes for you to shift from the need for perfection to a place of *realistic* goal-setting.
> 5. Once the answer at Step 2 is yes, then go ahead and do the task — but make sure you work to the realistic guidelines you have set.

Few things in life come without a cost. Striving to meet high standards can lead to great things but it can extract quite a price if we 'fail' to meet the goal. Consider the following:

- Have you ever taken the time to reflect upon your reactions and internal dialogue when you do not meet your goals?
- What happens to your emotions in situations where you come face to face with your 'imperfection' (as you might term it)?
- Do you allow yourself to enjoy or savour your achievements when you do succeed, or do you simply reset your standards even higher?

One of the things noted earlier was that the desire for a perfect outcome can lead to both procrastination and paralysis. So, just to balance things out a little, it appears that procrastination may not always be a recipe for disaster. It is rumoured that Mozart wrote the overture to *Don Giovanni* on the morning that the opera premiered ... and by all accounts that turned out all right!

8.
HEALTH AND WELLBEING

Throughout the book so far, we have acknowledged that both the hard working/driven and A/N personality styles can have significant benefits for the individual. This is in terms of financial reward, status acquired, promotions gained and useful connections made, as well as a personal sense of achievement and an enhanced sense of self. However, there is seldom anything that is totally pure and positive. Most of the time there are costs attached to or associated with anything that is rewarding. You make money on investments, but you pay more tax; you develop a taste for a sweet dessert, but your waistline increases!

Similarly, there tend to be costs associated with the non-stop, overly focused approach to work tasks and life in general. However, these costs are not always easily identified. If you are driven, this can be a trap because, as you will recall, one of the main personal attributes is the tendency to focus on the proximal — and potentially positive — outcomes. Rarely is much thought given to the delayed, negative outcomes (unless, of course, we tap into the fear of failure). By seeing the connection between hard work, long hours and personal talents, you regularly reinforce the behaviours that bring about the positives. As a result, you may continue on the road to success and tend not to notice the warning signs along the journey. These negative outcomes can, either singly or in combination, become a threat to the individual, their emotional and physical wellbeing, employment situation or family relationships. In this chapter, we shall therefore look at some of the potential challenges that can result from following a life that is out of balance and affected by burnout. Hopefully by being forewarned, you can be forearmed.

PHYSICAL HEALTH

Being healthy is a complex and multifaceted issue. It is not just about the status of one's muscles and bones and it does not depend solely on physical wellbeing. An important factor often overlooked by many people, and the medical world at large, is the role of personality structure and its effect on choices and behaviours. A high-achieving personality style can have both direct and indirect influences on how we view and relate to health, as well as how we interact with the medical world. This approach sets up a range of expectations, beliefs and responses that may be regularly reinforced through life.

The learning experiences that result in a driven or A/N personality style tend to promote stoicism and self-reliance. Therefore, if a doctor is consulted, it may be quite late in the piece due to the conflicting demands of work and other responsibilities. This can have implications for illness progression, as well as treatment options and outcomes. Once treatment has begun, there may also be a number of challenges for the work-oriented individual around following treatment protocols. This can range from the taking of medications through to attending medical appointments.

It has already been suggested that the learning experiences within family, school and work environments shape the perspectives of such individuals as they grow up. The family of origin may have, either subtly or clearly, demonstrated certain behaviours around health and this perhaps was reflected in parental responses to reports of feeling unwell and minor injury as the child developed. If the family valued performance and getting on with things, there may have been a high threshold to be met before outside assistance was sought. This is not to suggest that these parents were neglectful or dismissive of important health issues. Rather, part of the valued attribute of 'being in control' and coping may have been the ability to tolerate minor ailments and illnesses. Additionally, time off work may not have been something that was modelled in the family and therefore days off school may have been few and far between. This would reflect the parental expectations that one should get on and perform their duty or role, and only take time off in circumstances that 'really' require it. (I have more than one medical colleague who has sent a child to school with 'a sore arm', only to find out later that it was actually fractured!)

In some sense, we are talking about a family culture around health and decisions about accessing professional healthcare. This may have provided a template for learning what it means to be ill and when it is acceptable to be unwell or have time off from responsibilities. Such learning can have a bearing upon the future health behaviours of a child who grew up in such an environment.

PREVIOUSLY LEARNED ATTITUDES AFFECT YOUR HEALTH NOW

Health behaviours are what each of us does regarding health-related issues. They can include taking a break, using medication (over-the-counter or prescribed), doing exercises shown to us by a physiotherapist, going for X-rays or having surgery. Additionally, the messages around health that you identify as being appropriate and/or correct can directly impact decisions and behaviours related to your own health. It is therefore important for each of us to take some time to reflect on the messages we have picked up over time and which could now guide our own health-related behaviour.

The fact you are reading this book indicates you have at least some degree of identification with the experience of burnout or the A/N personality style. As such, you might have picked up some attitudes and expectations around health over the years and these could possibly now be guiding some of your behaviours and self-care approaches. If you can start to account for the potential impact of these early messages, there may be opportunities to better influence your health when necessary. However, it is also important to understand that such benefits are not just physical; they can have positive spin-offs for your psychological welfare and general quality of life as well. It may also have future financial benefit for you, as you start to consider the benefits of 'preventive maintenance' for your body. Staving off a heart attack or reducing blood pressure surely has considerable benefits for the future of both you and your family. It may also mean that you can continue working rather than having to prematurely retire or leave your job due to health issues. If you would like to make positive changes and challenge unhelpful health behaviours and attitudes, you might benefit from understanding the schemas and beliefs that promote certain ways of viewing and responding to your own health. By gaining an understanding of how these attitudes have impacted the way you care for yourself, you will be better placed to understand when these are coming into play. You should then be able to choose positive, helpful options for self-care, rather than automatically following a well-practised approach. Paradoxically, being off work due to burnout can actually afford you the time to reset your approach to health and wellbeing.

Some of the key schemas within the driven individual involve concerns around getting on with things, not letting pain or illness affect responsibilities, and the primacy of your work. These are powerful scripts to operate by. The primacy of your work can mean that one's own needs are relegated to the background. If you are a business executive there may be demands within the workday, an important contract that needs finetuning or ensuring that employee needs are met. Unfortunately, these may well take precedence over personal health status.

Obviously, a wide range of factors can and do influence health status. Part of this is our genetic make-up. Although there is not much we can do about our genetic inheritance, there may be options for us to better manage how we respond to what our genes might throw at us. If we can see that the health-related behaviours we undertake are modifiable, we may have an opportunity to reduce the impact of health problems or gain better outcomes from treatment. The important aspect for each of us is to realize that the decisions we take at any stage of the health cycle will be affected by the way each of us makes sense of and relates to what it means to be a busy, outcome-oriented person. If you strongly relate to this style of interacting with the world, you will be more likely to overlook minor ailments and less likely to find time to consult a doctor. The former may be due to the nuisance value of addressing non-urgent issues. The latter may be difficult due to competing demands such as work pressures/expectations and timing of appointments.

The degree to which one 'lives' the achievement-focused life can map indirectly onto healthcare use and the value placed on caring for oneself. If you are constantly busy with work (and the associated demanding schedules), there may be little room to engage in the aforementioned 'preventive maintenance'. Once you are caught up in this world, the expectations and beliefs of the associated culture may override physical needs. Once these external aspects are mapped onto the internalized expectations and beliefs, the stage is set for a long-term process of potentially riding through minor ailments, putting off consultations and clinical tests, as well as not having time to comply with treatment regimes. Such beliefs are often magnified by the ethos and expectations of the environment you operate in. If this is in a competitive workplace (think promotions, bonuses and achieving partnerships), there may be a significant amount of modelling around health behaviours. As you ascend the professional ladder, it will be noticed if you take time off due to illness. If deadlines need to be extended, there may be personal, work-related or even financial repercussions. Those outcomes are highly likely to influence future choices.

In some ways, if you are experiencing burnout you could be a victim of your own process, as far as awareness of health status goes. By not attending the doctor very often, the assumption is that all is well and you are healthy. This can be a self-sustaining issue that has implications when you do finally attend a health clinic. You might overlook other physical challenges that are not (yet) too problematic, as you wish to get the current issue addressed and return to what you are doing as quickly as possible. This is consistent with a work-prioritizing personality style and the demands of the workplace, which tend to favour the 'here and now' over the future, and being more oriented to the goal rather than the process. So, you might find yourself attending the doctor and seeking the quickest intervention, to address the problem (e.g.

a pill to 'fix' the issue). The idea of listening to or complying with changes to diet, exercise or general health-management advice probably seems too much hassle. From the other side of the desk, the clinician may be at risk of operating on a form of shorthand due to your history of attendance and possible minimization of symptoms. This can set up a 'false positive' paradigm, where both patient and clinician see the encounter within the context of a healthy person. One of the dangers of this is that consultations tend to be shorter, fewer questions are asked and fewer preventive options provided. This is not necessarily because the doctor is uncaring or not doing their job. Rather, it can be a consequence of the history around attendance, the minimization of problems and symptoms (by the patient who 'needs' to get back to work) and the limited time available in consultations. For both parties, the assumption of wellness can mean certain courses of action are favoured over others.

Minimizing problems

Of course, it is a tall ask of the medical fraternity to identify a patient as operating within an overly focused or driven manner; more so to expect them to immediately realize that the way such a patient has learned to go about things will probably affect their descriptions of symptoms and timing of presentation. Therefore, it is important that you develop an understanding of factors relevant to how you view health and how you behave in response to your changing health status. I don't think it would be fair or appropriate to say that people with burnout do not care about their health. Similarly, it is probably not the case that, deep down, you are convinced that you are bullet-proof and super-human in terms of health. It is more likely that a range of schemas are operating that make it less likely that you will go to the doctor. It is also helpful to note that these may also be layered onto internal factors such as a tendency towards minimization, a degree of denial and not wishing to be seen as 'not in control'. We know that the latter is a particular risk for males.

The tendency to minimize problems is an interesting trait and one that can map easily onto the personality styles we are exploring in this book. It can perhaps be best seen as a coping strategy (albeit not always a helpful one), which is designed to underline a sense of being in control. If health issues are downplayed, this can be a way of ensuring you do not overreact or — worse still — be *seen* to be overreacting to physical problems. This reduces the psychological conflict around needing to be available for work but perhaps also wondering about consulting a doctor.

Benjamin is a busy professional who made one of his few visits to the doctor after having trouble breathing when training for a half-marathon. He gave a cursory account of the difficulties within the specific confines of the running environment and shared with the doctor his self-diagnosis of exercise-induced asthma. Benjamin then proceeded to explain to the doctor that his preferred approach would be to get an inhaler to deal with the symptoms when training. As someone who didn't like attending healthcare professionals and who begrudgingly admitted to viewing health problems as a personal failure, Benjamin wanted to get the problem sorted so he could return to his running.

The doctor offered the opinion that these symptoms were 'not too convincing of asthma', yet he acquiesced and provided the sought-after inhaler. This seems to have been a situation where one party was bringing certain A/N expectations and pressures to the consultation and this, when combined with the general presumption of good health (as crudely measured by attendance rates at the doctor), resulted in a treatment approach not necessarily favoured by the doctor.

In due course, Benjamin was back at the doctor with worsening symptoms that resulted in a referral to a cardiologist, with subsequent stenting being carried out!

In the medium to long term, this minimization is not useful or helpful. The real-life outcome can be that you encounter internal barriers to seeking timely and effective help. This can have consequences for yourself, your family, your workplace and the medical personnel who try to treat the problem when you do eventually attend for assistance. Invariably, the condition will have worsened or advanced, which can have implications for cost, prognosis and ... time off work (the very thing you were trying to avoid). Ironic, huh? So, minimization may well end up a rather costly strategy! If we stay with the case study involving cardiac symptoms, the implications for the status of the arteries and the potential for experiencing a heart attack may be significant. Not taking your symptoms seriously can have direct effects on future wellbeing and employment potential. I therefore encourage anyone with the traits described here to ask themselves: 'Why do I not go to the doctor?', 'Have I been prioritizing work over my health?', 'What is behind my tendency to minimize my symptoms?' It is perhaps time to look in the mirror and ask yourself honestly about what might be getting in the way of caring for yourself. It is possible that the reasons are rooted within the learned approach to life being outlined in this book.

As you can see, our learning and personality style potentially impact health status. It is probably true that some aspects of your personality style are more relevant than others. Further, it would also be true that some people who identify with a driven approach to life *do* prioritize their health status and care. This can be because good health is seen as vital to achieving the goal/s they are most focused upon; consider the team members of any Olympic sport that you follow. It may therefore be more about understanding when some aspects of your personality style are coming into play and also seeing how (and when) these affect your decision-making. How you make sense of your internal demands and view the expectations of those around you (e.g. the boss and other hard-working people) regarding health issues, may well affect the health-related behaviours you choose.

A final issue of physical relevance for driven individuals is the tendency to believe their body will inform them when they have reached their tolerance level. Unfortunately, people in the throes of burnout can become so focused on the goal of staying at work that they ignore, override, misinterpret or generally discount changes to the way they are feeling. This can see them pushing on, despite the fact their body is providing feedback that things are under stress. In its simplest form, this might be the development of a cold or feeling fatigued. However, at the other end of the spectrum this can be a significant illness or disease process. Unfortunately, many A/N or driven people only notice the feedback from their body — and take it as a message that something is wrong — when they struggle to carry on. Sounding a bit like when you reached the state of burnout, perhaps? Only then do they seem to consider that something might be affecting them or is out of balance. However, most probably there has been a feedback loop operating from the body for quite some time. It just hasn't been attended to. Time to change this, perhaps?

PSYCHOLOGICAL HEALTH

There are a number of psychological health effects (short term and longer) that can flow from the experience of burnout. We will now explore low mood, depression and anxiety. These can be a consequence of burnout but can also be contributors to its development. It may therefore be helpful to understand how these present and their effects on you.

Low mood and depression

It is not unusual for people who push themselves to experience alterations to their mood. As the demands of work or general life build up, there can be implications for how people feel about themselves and a particular situation. Within the general population, depression is a relatively common disorder. It is, however, a truth that depression is not always recognized by many of the people involved, including the individuals themselves, the doctor who may be consulted and family members and friends. This can particularly occur with those who might be termed 'high functioning' depressed people — a group that could well include more than its fair share of driven individuals like yourself.

Everyone experiences a range of emotions and this includes low mood due to frustrations, losses and upsetting events. Some of these lowered moods may be characterized more appropriately as sadness and grief, while others might be more of a reactive lowering in response to events. On top of this, though, there can be what is termed a major depressive episode. This is a clinical condition involving a lowered mood that is present nearly every day and can be accompanied by a reduced interest in usually enjoyable activities and a drop in motivation.

Alongside this, there can be a range of physical effects associated with the condition. In more pronounced cases, this can also result in thoughts about death and self-harm. This is by no means a full and complete checklist for major depression, but it gives an idea of some of the changes that come about when a person's mood lowers consistently.

There is no single reason or event that results in or causes depression in everyone who experiences it. Indeed, there can be a range of events and situations that contribute components to a person's significant change in mood. These may be a genetic vulnerability (a family history traced through a number of sufferers) and/or the presence of ongoing stressful events such as work demands, relationship and financial issues. Such issues can be compounded by a change in thinking style that accompanies lowered mood and results in the person adopting a more negative view of life and events.

Depression is not a 'one size fits all' problem. So if this condition is relevant, you might need some help to make sense of what is happening for you and some advice on the options available. One of the most important messages for anyone who has become burnt out is that depression is not a failing, nor is it indicative of weakness. I point this out as some people experiencing burnout have issues around control and a fear of failure. Associated with this is a mistaken view within general society that only 'weak' people become depressed. Similarly, there is often a misunderstanding and fear that only weak people experience burnout. As a practising clinical psychologist I can assure you that people from all walks of life and socio-economic backgrounds present with mood-related challenges.

There is no singly identifiable person who presents with this condition, and it is neither fair nor accurate to describe depressed people as being weak-willed or having a compromised character. Some of my clients who have struggled with their mood hold very responsible positions in large organizations. It is also really important for you to know that most people recover sufficiently from a depressive episode to return to their general lives.

An appropriate first port of call would be to talk with your family doctor. Remember, there is no need to feel shame at becoming depressed. As we have seen, there are a range of reasons why this can develop. For the person with burnout, these can include the continuous pressures and stressors of performing at high levels in their chosen field. Alongside this may have been the constant presence of that unhelpful passenger, the harsh internal critic, who has freely imparted negative messages about your performance and abilities in general. It is a truth that even healthy, fit and dedicated people can wear themselves out — physically and psychologically.

If your partner or doctor has identified changes to your mood, it might be time to pause and listen. As noted, the first step is to see a professional who can help with the diagnosis and provide either direct assistance or a referral to another professional with appropriate specialist training. There are also any number of self-help books and materials available from bookshops and websites. A complete discussion around the role of antidepressants is beyond the scope of this book. However, I would like you to be open to talking through all options with your medical or mental health professional if the need arises. By fully informing yourself about all options, you will hopefully be better placed to make the decisions about your health and welfare that you need to make.

There is a significant body of research-based evidence around the benefits of talking-based therapies for mood problems. One of the best-known approaches within this is cognitive behavioural therapy (CBT), which helps you understand the factors that have contributed to the current depressive episode while providing a range of strategies to manage your symptoms. For our purposes, it is important to understand that pushing yourself (both physically and mentally) while being hard on yourself and dismissive of achievements can have a detrimental effect upon your mood. This, in turn, can undermine your confidence and impact your performance in the role you are connected with, value so highly or have become trapped in. Hopefully, by understanding the key issues within this chapter you will develop an awareness of signs and symptoms that indicate your mood is lowering. As a result, you may be able to respond in a timely manner to prevent the problems compounding and making things increasingly difficult for you.

Anxiety

Okay, let's be upfront from the start: anxiety is a bitch of a condition. It is also an issue of potential relevance to people with burnout — current or developing. This can lurk around in the shadows of depression and quietly sneak up, or it can be a challenge within its own right. This condition is about being 'unsure' and includes quite a few questions of the 'What if …?' type. This is very relevant for those who want to or 'need' to achieve. Anxiety can result in you second-guessing yourself and living in a heightened state of arousal, where the worst-case scenario seems the most obvious outcome. It tends to undermine your sense of control and may reinforce the nagging doubts that maybe, just maybe 'I am a fraud after all'.

Anxiety is a busy condition. It has several components that can have a specific or cumulative effect on the individual. These are an emotional response; a physical response; unhelpful and worrying thoughts; and changes to how we behave (i.e. we tend to avoid the things we are anxious about). Anxiety is a basic defence mechanism that developed in humans a long time ago, when we were living in caves and eating woolly mammoth steaks for dinner. It is essentially about keeping ourselves safe by quickly getting ready for threats within our world. The aim of anxiety is to rev up the system to respond to a potential threat. It does this by getting the body ready to either do battle with the threat or hot-foot it away from the scene of the threat. This is known as the fight or flight response, which produces useful physical changes that assist us to deal with the threat. Most noticeably, the fight or flight response involves pumping blood to the major muscle groups to give them oxygen in readiness for action. As part of this, our breathing becomes faster (and shallower) and our heart rate increases alongside a tensing of certain muscle groups. By doing this, and by releasing adrenaline, the person then has a better chance of responding to a threat and hopefully looking after themselves. These responses are common throughout the animal kingdom and, let's face it, we humans are also animals when all is said and done.

This defence mechanism was designed for a simpler, more physical age but we still carry it with us in the 21st century. It is still necessary and not something you can completely rid yourself of — so don't waste your time and energy trying. But while eliminating anxiety is a bridge too far, managing it is definitely possible. Have you noticed how our world has become more complex, socialized and technologically driven? This means that with the busy brains we have developed, we can now get anxious about things that are not physical threats; in fact, the 'threat' does not even have to be associated with immediate events. Our specialized brains have enabled us to imagine and project ahead (or back) in time. This means that we can become anxious about social interactions and potential difficulties and threats. The relevance of this to people with burnout is that humans can become anxious about potential failure and the potential responses of others to our (perceived) failings and poor performance. Anxiety becomes more of a problem when we anticipate future problems and when such concerns become consistent or second nature. This results in an ongoing state of heightened emotional, physical and cognitive arousal, which is not helpful or efficient.

Our systems respond in this manner whether the danger is real or perceived. The individual becomes increasingly alert and starts to scan the environment (social or work-based) for variations of the threat, and for any new ones. Because our system is then primed for action, it doesn't take much to trigger a response of fleeing or responding in an attacking manner. Within a social setting, this can see an anxious person leave the environment or say something they may later regret. Due to the fact the alarm system is ringing loud and clear, the focus is on dealing with the perceived threat and not much thought goes into the consequences of our actions. This can be costly in an employment situation where one may verbally attack another due to the perceived threat — not good if the recipient is your boss!

When anxious, our thinking becomes less sophisticated, with a much narrower focus (i.e. dealing only with the threatening situation that is here and now). Thoughts focus on being in some kind of 'danger' and we tend to consider the worst-case scenario regarding the outcome. This is important for the work-focused individual, as you can 'learn' that unfamiliar situations, such as not meeting a goal or deadline, are threatening. This can result in an increase in effort and energy expenditure, beyond the already high levels, in order to stave off potential failure. Alternatively, it might result in further procrastination or avoidance. Living in a state of uncertainty and wondering if or when things will go wrong will quietly but surely wind up your nervous system, undermine confidence and potentially heighten the fear of failure that may be lurking beneath the surface. It can also play havoc with your sense of peace within your home life and undermine your confidence within previously enjoyed and managed activities.

A special word about worry

As you are no doubt aware, burnout leaks out into all aspects of your life. Even if you have resigned or taken leave from work, the effects will continue until you are able to gain a foothold on the symptoms and bring them under control. As noted above, anxiety can be a part of burnout, due to the uncertain nature of what is happening and why. Unfortunately, the heightened arousal in your nervous system can continue across all domains of your life. One of the major intrusions resulting from this is the tendency to worry. This can be focused upon one aspect (e.g. your performance at work) or it can become quite generalized (e.g. your future, your children's wellbeing, or the state of the nation). This generalized aspect is incredibly unhelpful, as it robs you of the chance to settle and enjoy your life.

Because we can't always predict the outcome of a situation, it adds fuel to the concern and we can expend a lot of negative emotional energy going over and over (and over) all aspects of the scenario that faces us. The act of worrying is a cognitive process and it involves thinking (usually negatively) about possible difficulties, unknowns or threats that may lie ahead of us. One of the things that keeps this uncertainty and anxiety alive is the fact that we cannot control events we do not fully understand or feel we don't have enough information about. So worrying is an attempt to bring about some control by working through all the possible solutions and management options. By doing this, we hope there will be a reduction in the feelings of uncertainty and the associated distress.

Worry is essentially a costly negative activity, in terms of using up valuable personal resources. Interestingly, there is evidence to show that some people who engage in worrying may have a positive belief about the cognitive action they are taking. They think that worrying will potentially help them to find a solution (i.e. to cope with whatever the threatening issue is) or somehow stop the feared outcome from eventuating. Unfortunately, things don't tend to work out like this. Worrying does not solve anything. Let me repeat that: *worrying does not solve anything*. All it will do is make you tired and suck your emotional energy without fixing the uncertainty.

Part of the problem is that responding to uncertainty by worrying serves to bring the threat more into focus and shifts your attention to potential risks and negative outcomes. Worry is associated with and impacts the way you view problems in front of you. This negative perspective can then flow into reduced problem-solving abilities. Unfortunately, this can leave you feeling powerless and overwhelmed by the situation confronting

Health and wellbeing

you. Due to a lack of learning or mastery developing, you are more likely to revert to the unhelpful (but familiar) tactics of worry and avoidance in the future — thus maintaining the vicious cycle associated with uncertainty and feelings of being overwhelmed.

> ### TRY THIS
>
> Worry awareness involves getting a sense of the extent you engage in worrying. If you don't know you have a problem (i.e. worrying) you won't be able to respond to it and help yourself.
>
> Consider setting an alarm on your phone to go off every 40 minutes. At that tone, stop whatever you are doing (if it is safe to do so) and note down what you were thinking about at the time of the alarm. (Hint: set the alarm to begin at something like twelve minutes past the hour. That way, the alarms will go off at times you are not expecting. On the hour will result in your brain realizing when the alarm is going to go off and this could affect what you are thinking about and distort the information you are trying to obtain.) At the end of the day, read though the outlines you noted down and see if there are any themes — especially repeating ones.
>
> Do this for a couple of days to establish the extent of your worrying. If it is happening quite a bit, follow any of the options below that suit you:
> - Establish whether the issue you are worrying about is something that can be sorted or eliminated. If it can, then follow an approach that employs your problem-solving skills. If it is something you do not have any influence over,

remind yourself that there is no point in using your energy to constantly go over the issue in your mind. Remember, though, that having some influence may mean that a degree of change to/with the issue is possible. There might be some things you can do to reduce the size of the problem or lessen the impact to a more manageable degree.

- Bring yourself back to the here and now by using grounding techniques or mindfulness approaches. Worry is about the past or the future, not the present.
- Distract yourself by giving your mind other things to focus on. This can help break or loosen the cycle associated with the worry. You could read a book or magazine, get out into the garden and do something there, listen to music or watch TV. Be aware, though, that if you don't work through the issues at the heart of the worry, you may end up trying to be busy and distracted all day long. If the worrying has been around for some time, perhaps have a prepared list of activities and tasks handy that you could try. This can help get around your mind going blank and leaving you feeling as if there is nothing you can do.
- Try delaying the worry. This can bring about a sense of control and efficacy in relation to the act of worrying. If the worries show up at weird and wonderful times, acknowledge them for what they are and tell yourself you have a time set aside to work with the worries (see below). You don't

need to focus on them just because they have been triggered by something or randomly decide to show up. Outside of that time, you are free to focus on other, more relevant issues and topics.
- Don't fight the act of worrying. Instead, consider corralling it or keeping it to a level that means it does not intrude on your life and functioning. This can be achieved by setting aside time to worry. Remember, you're not trying to ignore, fight or run from worry. Worry time involves you picking a time when you are going to sit down and give yourself permission to be present with the worries. However, this is best done at a predetermined time that suits you and doesn't intrude on other activities, rather than grabbing a moment when the worries arise. Give it some boundaries, though; for example, allow yourself fifteen to twenty minutes to worry and go over the issues. Set a timer so you know when the opportunity is up for the day. You can spend the time thinking about the topic, or you could write the worries down as a way of processing any thoughts and feelings. This time may also be a chance to check out the worries by considering whether they are realistic or as big as they seem when they appear in your head. This might just offer the chance to see things a different way. Once the time is up, get back to whatever is normal, usual or important for you.
- Journalling is popular with some people. This isn't about obsessively writing down everything about the worries. Rather, it can be a positive way to

> express how you are feeling and 'get out' the issues you are concerned about. You might even try noting down some possible solutions or positive responses to the worries — a sort of brainstorming session in a controlled setting. This may help to bring about a differing view on the issue and you might be able to see that the threat is not as big as you thought.
> - Don't forget the use of excellent skills such as breathing techniques, relaxation, meditation and mindfulness practices. These can help to give both your mind and body a break from the stress and tension associated with worrying.

TO SUM UP

When work takes over your life and begins to dominate all aspects of your world, it can have major costs — not the least of which is burnout. As some of these costs are delayed, you might not notice they are building up. As the driven or A/N person tends to focus on the project or task at hand, they tend not to look ahead and this can limit their ability to care for themself. There can also be competing demands from prioritized tasks such as work, which can delay a person seeking help with health problems.

Part of being overly committed is having a low tolerance to things that don't work out. If you see health problems as a failing, or view addressing these as an acknowledgement of weakness, then your chances of actively addressing health problems is lessened. Minimizing your symptoms and problems will not make them go away; in fact, it may well make things harder in the longer term. If you relate to this pattern, now is the time to start rebalancing things in your life. After all, you can't do well in your chosen field or return to your role if the body is not able to perform as well as it can.

Health issues, illness, depression and anxiety are *not* failures. You are human, despite your strengths and achievements. Ask yourself: what other machine have you run (often at peak performance) every day for 30, 40, 50 or more years? Do you expect all the machinery and devices you have purchased to last for this length of time without demonstrating some problems or needing some servicing?

A chance for change

Being yourself — rather than who you think you should be or feel you are expected to be — is an important step in managing your health and coming out the other side of burnout. If you act in ways that feel real and genuine for you, it is more likely you will be accounting for important aspects of your wellbeing. There is a strong relationship between happiness, feeling less stressed, doing well at work and engaging in life in a style consistent with your personal values. It should not be just about fitting everything in with your goals.

In terms of your overall self, take some time to consider how you relate to your physical wellbeing and health. Ask yourself what's behind the decisions you take, and have taken, about your health. Why are you putting off going to the doctor for a check-up? What might be the long-term outcome of such behaviours, for you, your career, your partner or your children?

What if you started to view your doctor in a similar vein as your business mentor or valued colleague? Consider seeing them as someone who can provide advice or help you address problems that might be undermining your progress. Let go of the view that the doctor is someone you only go to once your body has 'failed' or broken down.

In terms of your psychological health, be assured that it is possible to expand your repertoire of management strategies. However, the first step is to realize you may be facing a challenge. If you can relate to the symptoms of worry, anxiety or depression listed earlier in the chapter, *now* is the time to do something about them. If you are not sure, show this chapter to your partner, best friend or a family member and ask them if they think the symptoms are relevant to you. Below are some specific things you can do right now:

- Talk with someone in the first instance, such as a family member or friend.
- Consult your family doctor.
- Be open to the option of medications (e.g. antidepressants) if advised.
- Consider participating in some talking therapy (e.g. CBT) with a psychologist.

Learn more about stress management and how to enhance any strategies you currently have in place. There are many good self-help books available, or you could talk with an accredited counsellor or psychologist. Skills they can help you with include problem-solving approaches, options for dealing with unhelpful cognitions (worry), diaphragmatic breathing, relaxation techniques, meditation, mindfulness skills, tai chi (it's okay, men; the moves were originally martial arts techniques!).

Burnout is not inevitable. Part of the secret to keeping it at bay relates to your motivation for the task and where it comes from. There are protective aspects to being motivated by your

Health and wellbeing

own reasons and values rather than by external factors or payoffs. If you are working towards goals and outcomes that are relevant and consistent with your values (more about values later), there is less chance you will become overwhelmed and then burn out. This intrinsic drive and reasoning will help you sustain effort when things get tough. This is because the goals are consistent with who you are and what is important to you — that is, they are not simply related to reinforcers such as increased money or respect from others. There is also an association between intrinsically identified goals and enhanced feelings of personal wellbeing, a positive sense of self and confidence for doing things.

So, what is it that drives you in your current (or recent) role: to do the best job you can, or to be famous? And where does the reinforcement come from: within you, or from other people or things outside of you? Be honest with yourself as you answer these questions.

TRY THIS

To make some change to this sphere of your life, consider just what was the original motivation for you in relation to your recent role and your performance in it. Write down the answers to the following questions:
- What drew you towards this role or activity in the first place?
- Why and how closely did this initially fit with your personal desires and values?
- Is there anything about the way you currently approach your role or activity that could be changed so that it might fit more closely with your personal desires and values?

> **Helpful hint:** If you are an employer or supervisor, be aware that role and workload can be perceived either as a taxing demand or a positive challenge by your employees and colleagues. As you can see from this chapter, what an individual brings to the workplace or team environment can have a significant bearing on their ability to cope with the tasks set for them. It may be advantageous to consider this when selecting individuals for roles in your organization. If you select people whose values, aptitudes and skills (not just conscientious behaviour) are congruent with the role in question, this should help them positively identify with the role. Therefore, they may be more likely to engage with the role, rather than feel dominated or stressed by it. As a result, they could find that they enjoy their role more, and this can often translate to better performance (plus reduce the chance of burnout).

As you understand more about burnout and the A/N approach to life and consider making some positive changes, think about this: what if you tried to shape your career-related behaviours around a refreshed, more meaningful approach to life ... as opposed to shaping your life around your career? This is the direction we will now explore together.

9.
NEW PERSPECTIVES, ACHIEVEMENT AND THE 'ME'

Change is central to adaptation, and adaptation is central to the successful mastery of a situation. As Darwin pointed out many years ago, it is the species that adapts to the demands of the environment that stands the best chance of successfully carrying on. If we are to make the most of opportunities, we will get more traction by adapting to changes or new expectations within our environment (e.g. our workplace or life outside of work) and after the problematic employment experience.

However, to see (and therefore benefit from) alternatives, we must be able to shift perspective when needed. Perhaps even more useful is the ability to weigh up options and then implement the most advantageous response. The opposite approach revolves around perseveration of ideas and behaviours. This will invariably lead to a sense of 'stuckness' and, in the extreme, helplessness. The latter is when you have the sense that there is no point trying anymore because nothing seems to work. Unfortunately, living with burnout for any length of time can take you to such a place.

In essence, adaptability is about choosing the most useful response at a given time. This is the one that maximizes your chances of coping with the situational demands, with minimal drain on your resources. Thus, you can adapt and adjust as needed without just relying on a 'full on' or 'full off' response set. As we have seen already, the default option of the work-focused (and A/N) person to challenging situations is to respond with a set of behaviours that revolve around putting in more hours and demanding more of themselves. If this sounds like you, it is possible you are identifying a bit too much with your 'tried and true' methods, which can lead to an overdeveloped belief in their usefulness. In such situations, you might find yourself acting on autopilot. This can result in you no longer actively considering how things are shaping up or changing, because you experience a narrowing of your focus. This may then impact your ability to monitor and regulate the extent of your dedication to the task.

PSYCHOLOGICAL FLEXIBILITY

Be water, my friend.
—BRUCE LEE

One branch of the psychological therapies that promotes flexibility as central to a healthy existence is acceptance and commitment therapy, or ACT. This very practical and useful approach endeavours to take account of the context for an individual and their behaviours. An introduction to this approach is contained in a 2006 paper by Hayes and his colleagues. One of their aims was to help the person build a wider repertoire of coping options, with an emphasis on flexibility. This school of thought emphasizes that, when we get too involved with and wrapped up in our thoughts, we risk controlling our behaviour through pre-existing rules and the thoughts themselves. By behaving like this, driven people may end up acting (automatically) in a way that is consistent with a strong focus on achievement at any cost. This can mean they miss out on the bigger picture that offers some balance and flexibility. This is certainly representative of those with burnout, in that you may live an increasingly narrow life which, over time, unwittingly distances you from the things previously held to be important. The goals, tasks and requirements of your professional role and associated projects take precedence. As a result, you could tend to rely increasingly on a restricted number of approaches to life and its problems (e.g. you push yourself harder, as that is what is 'expected' or 'all I can do about it'). This can become a rather circular process, whereby you can see no option but to carry on as you have and, because these approaches are familiar (even though you know they are not helping you), you carry on using them which means you no longer look for other ways or approaches. You know how you often go to the same supermarket, at the same time each week, along the same route? Well, guess what? There are other supermarkets in your neighbourhood and there are other routes you can take to your current one.

Psychological flexibility is about being open (within yourself) to experiences and possibilities. This can help you to see options and begin to consider differing perspectives, which will help you with the change process and adaptability mentioned above. It is more helpful to generate a range of ways to approach a given situation than to stop at the first idea or 'solution'. I guess we are talking about enhancing your ability to work with and adapt how you think about or respond to a situation. If you are unable to operate via differing options, you are more likely to plug in the well-rehearsed and accepted approaches. This is particularly so within a work environment, which has routines and expectations.

I would like to encourage you to start questioning your initial responses to situations, settings and tasks. This can be as simple as gently saying, 'Okay, that's my first thought, what else could I do here?' or 'Yeah, that's how I have always responded to that request but what else could I say?'. I am not suggesting you begin to doubt yourself. Rather, this is about pausing after the automatic thoughts/responses you have and then asking (not demanding) if there is another way to view things. The benefit of this is a developing awareness that there may be choices available and some of these may actually be better for you.

Your brain is just like mine: it likes efficiency. However, sometimes it trades off the consideration of alternatives for the ease of repeating the same approach. This is the result of learning, repetition and sometimes fear of the consequences of change. Despite this, our brains can become more open and available to differing perspectives — much like your muscles and limbs can grow and perform differently as a result of new exercises or stretching. The benefit for you, as you try to move away from living in a state of burnout, is that you can take your cognitive resources and abilities and use them for things that are more positive, helpful or that fit better with how you want your life to look going forward. Where once you would have responded by prioritizing work tasks, you might now find yourself better able to see that time with your children or partner could be more rewarding and meaningful. Here, I like the notion of choice — that is, now you see there are options, you can pick the one that fits with where you are at, what you are interested in or would prefer. This is coming from within you, not the same old, externally driven and determined series of events that have a (now) predictable outcome. If you can see there is a choice in how you react, you simply do not have to slavishly follow what you have always done.

A key to operating in this more flexible manner is to be aware of what you are encountering — not what you think it is or how you think it should be. This is a more positive type of focus than the driven, targeted approach we have been discussing so far. Here, I am suggesting that you consciously pay attention to what you encounter, no matter how many times you have seen it before. Familiarity is the key ingredient of shortcuts! By attending to and asking yourself what is in front of you, you have a better chance of considering options outside your usual, repeating approach. Shortcuts promote speed and effectiveness but they also trap you into repeating the unhelpful behaviours that led to burnout in the first place. As part of this change to how you respond, I encourage you to ask yourself just what is needed to meet the task at hand, and then (pause, breathe and consider before acting) just how much of your available resources are required at this time. Remember, your automatic approach has probably involved a full-on response set. The identification of what this task, on this occasion, in front of you now needs (in order to achieve a successful outcome) allows you to titrate your behaviours — and hopefully keep something in the tank for later.

TRY THIS

Here are some tips for kickstarting flexible thinking:
- Mix up your morning routines and actions — do things in a different order.
- Change the route you go on your evening walk.
- Try occasionally buying your petrol from a different place.

> - Be spontaneous with activities in your day.
> - Approach common tasks in a new/different way — e.g. mow your lawn in straight lines as opposed to the usual circles

If you can become more flexible in how you see the world, you will hopefully see that you do not have to do the same things, in the same way, all the time. You can adjust and adapt your approach to work, leisure and relationships. If these have all become predictable and repetitive, with less-than-exciting outcomes, it may well be time to try a different approach. The key maintaining factors we have looked at in earlier chapters rely on your same-same approach for their very existence. You don't need to buy the same patterned curtains each time you move house. If you consider the new environment, colourings and lighting, you may well come up with a new option that better suits your new home and gives a whole new feel; one that promotes and brings about a greater sense of contentment or comfort.

GOALS DRIVE YOU, BUT VALUES CAN GUIDE YOU

One of the things I consider useful about the ACT approach is that it tries to reconnect people with the things that are truly important to them. Within this, the approach tries to help the person align their behaviour so it is consistent with and guided by their values. This helps each of us to move toward wider ranging, more positive outcomes from our actions. Flexibility will flow more easily if your behaviours and choices fit with and are guided by your personal values. Surely it is more comfortable (and less threatening) to change direction, if we feel this is taking us somewhere that is valued and meaningful.

There may well be room for you to reconnect with your personal values. These aren't ancient, lost artifacts that you need to mount a huge expedition to dig up. Rather, they are more like misplaced personal treasures that have sat at the back of the cupboard for some time — a little bit dusty perhaps, but still precious and useful. Once you come across them again, you will start to see there can be different ways to do life and participate in work. This can, in turn, lead to a more meaningful, healthier self.

Values are those aspects you feel are important in terms of your direction in life, and perhaps what you wish your life to be about or would like it to reflect. If you can clarify these, then the values might operate as signposts for life, particularly during times when the journey becomes challenging. As such, these values may be able to motivate or even inspire you to act in ways that fit with what you hold to be important, rather than what you feel is required (e.g. reaching the top of your chosen career, at any cost). They can also act as guidance mechanisms for a pathway out of burnout. This involves clarifying what really is important for you and getting in touch with key principles that might guide you. If you are a parent, for example, this might be concerned with how you want to interact with and relate to your children — the style of communication through which you want to connect, the way you express your affection or the personal qualities you want to show and live by. The flow on is that the choices you make can be touched by your values and result in behaviours that are more fitting with the real you — as opposed to those well-rehearsed, automatic patterns of doing.

Goals versus values

This, of course, does not mean that those who have experienced burnout do not have any values. Rather, as a result of their driven personality and the stressors of what they have been through, they often focus on goals. *Goals are not the same as values* and learning the difference may open a window of opportunity for change. Goals are things you aim for, that can be achieved and then get ticked off from the lists that you are so good at generating. There is no lack of ability within the driven person to set and then work towards goals. If anything, this skillset has become overdeveloped and, in the process of enhancing this, there has been some loss in terms of accounting for personal values.

Values are a reflection and expression of the principles that are important to you and which act as your guide through life, if you connect with them. Consider what it might be like to participate in your (existing or new) job in a way that is consistent with the positive, helpful beliefs and approaches that are central to who you want to be. What if you could approach your tasks guided by values around shared participation, for example, and demonstrating your personal qualities, as opposed to your skills?

However, you don't need to choose either goals *or* values. It is just that one of these tends to dominate things for work and career focused people. This may see you setting goals for a career 'pathway' and then resetting them (higher) once you have achieved the aim. There tends to be no problem for such folk in following a clear process to ensure that they are able to meet their goals, in a timely and capable manner. Have you heard about setting SMART goals? Of course, you have. This approach was great in terms of helping you learn to set goals for efficiency and to maximize the chances of achieving them. However, in my clinical experience, high-achieving people know this stuff and have been to numerous workshops on many variations of SMART goal-setting. Rather than go down that road again, it may be important to acknowledge that your goal-setting skills are at an optimal/acceptable level. Perhaps it is now time to balance this with other strategies and learn how to account for important factors such as personal values. For, in essence, it is the balancing aspect of the overall equation that is underdone if you are driven or high achieving. To help you obtain this balance, consider reconnecting with your values in order to account for other important aspects that are relevant to your unbalanced world. Those values might relate to family and personal relationships, and positive steps might include re-establishing friendships that have slipped away over time or re-exploring some cultural, artistic or recreational aspect you once enjoyed or highly prized.

Identifying your values

In the spirit of the above, why not take a few moments to do a Google search on 'values lists'. Choose one to show you the range and type of values that can be part of you and your world. From this, perhaps select six values that strongly resonate with you. What might it mean for you if you can reconnect with them and bring these values to the forefront, as you think about moving forward with your life? How might you approach your current or future employment role if you allow these to guide you and your behaviours?

AN EMPTY SPACE

If you suffer from burnout or have an A/N personality, you might fear what could happen if you slow down or take time for yourself. Unfortunately, the automatic image generated from this notion of slowing down is often one of wasted time, empty space, self-indulgence and possibly not knowing what to do with the extra time. Remember, time and space have been successfully filled for a long time now by the focus on your chosen pursuit or career. The notion of not having something to work on can be, quite simply, scary. It is also unsettling as most people who push themselves find it hard to generate options that they could do if they weren't so busy. This is not the same as never having had any other dimensions to your personality, nor does it suggest that you have previously led a shallow and empty life. Rather, it is an indication of how much you have focused on particular issues, goals and tasks, often to the exclusion of things you once gained enjoyment and positive reinforcement from. I would like to suggest that you now need to revisit things from the past and reconfigure your sense of self around what was once valued. Considering this can be like those illuminated emergency strips on the floor of the aircraft that you never noticed until the aircrew pointed them out. Just as these strips can guide you to the exit (and safety) during an emergency, so can newly observed values act as a guiding pathway out of the negative space that is burnout.

This 'new' approach to life is about helping you reorient your perspective, identify what you would like to do (rather than *have* to do) and consider how you might prefer to spend your 'spare' time. This can be an important step towards starting to tap into what is meaningful for you as an individual, rather than useful as a team member. Consider for just an instant: if you had spare time, time that wasn't related to finishing a project or moving towards completion of a goal, how would you act? What would you do differently and why? A relevant part of this process is looking at the positive changes that may come about. It is also about seeing this as an ongoing, active and sustainable aspect, as you clarify how you want to engage with the world. Reconnecting with your values is not a destination or a chance to publicly say, 'I have certain values.' Rather, it is about identifying and relating to things that may well become signposts for your new journey in life. You might not have previously called them values. They may just have been things that inspired you towards a course of action or ways you acted because it felt 'right' or 'good'.

Of course, nothing in life is as simple as just deciding, 'I am going to change.' You can bet anything you like that, upon considering a change, your mind will immediately throw up reasons why this won't work or how change may disrupt important and relevant issues already on the go. Such blocking is a result of the intense focus on tasks and ways of viewing life that have elevated goal attainment (and actions in pursuit of this) to the highest of levels. If you feel, however, that it is time to try to change, then get in touch with what is meaningful for you, rather than what is productive or efficient. As you get the hang of this 'strange' and unfamiliar approach to life, you might start to notice a subtle change in some of the language that runs through your head. No longer will it all be about 'I have to' or 'I must'. Now it might be about 'I would like to', 'That might be fun' or 'I wonder what might happen if ...'. This could be the beginning of a voyage of discovery or, more accurately, a renewed exploration, with different eyes and focus, of the worlds you already move within.

ACCEPTANCE EQUALS GIVING UP ... OR DOES IT?

Alongside the concept of flexibility sits the very useful and almost 'kind' approach of acceptance. This concerns a person's readiness to experience, and thereby increase their capacity to tolerate, things that feel uncomfortable. In particular, this approach is relevant to the internal appraisals and beliefs, which are often about the self and performance. As already mentioned, difficulties meeting goals are often interpreted as a failing, rather than a challenge to be overcome. If that sounds familiar, you could benefit from learning to tolerate the associated unpleasant emotional experiences and the unhelpful memories that tend to come flooding in once a challenge is encountered.

If you struggle to accept this common human aspect of life (i.e. a less-than-perfect performance), then you may be at risk of heightened sensitivity to emotional difficulties. In particular, this could see anxiety and depression becoming a problem. However, the very issue of acceptance is a double-edged sword for most people who push themselves. It does not come naturally, and discussing the concept of acceptance tends to bring up connotations of defeat. To 'accept' something is interpreted as it having beaten you, and that you cannot find a solution. Therefore, it embodies images of rolling over and acknowledging that 'I have failed'. Rather than use the term acceptance, I tend to phrase the idea as 'accommodating' to the presence of unfamiliar emotions and/or uncomfortable states and situations that cannot be 'fixed' but that need to be worked alongside or managed.

Once the scene is set and language agreed upon, it is time to explore what 'accommodation' might actually mean for you as someone who has been living with burnout. In essence, this is not an abandoning of control. Rather, it embodies flexibility around being okay with some unsettling emotional states and not fearing them. If you can come to tolerate the presence of some worry and doubt, you might find it is possible to draw on a wider range of behaviours and responses that are not solely related to controlling the feelings. It will be helpful for you to learn that you can 'surf' your way through some levels of internal discomfort and, at other times, you can respond with strategies to manage the uncomfortable arousal you are experiencing. This is accommodating to the presence of naturally occurring and understandable emotional responses to those challenging situations. Although these feelings may be unsettling to the usually confident and dynamic, driven person, they are not in and of themselves pathological states. Indeed, a case could be made that ignoring or denying such experiences may actually lead you along the road to pathology!

You do not need to be 'cured' of unhelpful thinking styles or emotional responses to disappointment. Perhaps it is okay for these thoughts, beliefs and ways of viewing the world to be present? The issue isn't 'Did they pop up?' but rather 'Did I automatically respond to them in ways I did not fully appreciate or account for?' A better place to be is to allow these automatic thoughts and feelings to appear but be comfortable with the fact they can be fleeting responses, and then discriminate between the more (or less) helpful ones, relevant to the circumstance and time. Is this thought or belief going to help or hinder me? In essence, being able to be with these thoughts and feelings, without slavishly implementing the automatic behaviours that often follow, is an example of accommodation (or acceptance) and flexibility.

'I missed the deadline; I'm not up to it so I need to work much harder and faster' — in truth, this sort of statement holds little validity. The problem is that emotionally driven behaviour is seldom well thought through. A better option, perhaps, is to put the emphasis upon behaving in the most effective way, in the current set of circumstances, with this particular set of contingencies. Notice how the emphasis here is shifting to the present, to what is happening *now*, and encouraging effective responding. Although this probably seems different to the stereotypical manner of responding that you are used to, such an approach is actually speaking a language that can resonate with your achievement-oriented personality. It is about effectiveness and efficiency — key words that you might relate and aspire to.

WHAT'S IN A PERSPECTIVE?

You might be able to see from the above that we are talking about a personal perspective on internal events, and this notion can help us understand — and, more importantly, address — some of the traps the consistently hardworking person can fall into. Getting a handle on the 'me' that is involved in relating to our place in the world can help to bring about a new perspective and assist us to see what might be better and different, as we escape the grip of burnout. This is particularly related to the sense of who and what we are. This approach suggests that, over time, we come to relate to the person in the mirror as embodying and representing all the attributes that we have developed.

As a way of explaining this, McCracken and Velleman describe the 'conceptualized self' as being our image of who we are, based on and built up from the attributes and stories of our life journey. The problem, as they point out, with this conceptualized self is that we can become strongly (and possibly non-discriminatingly) attached to its associated story. This can result in the development of the previously mentioned rigidity. In essence, there is a shorthand operating each time we see ourselves in the mirror and reflect upon who we are. This underscores the notion that *this* is who I am, who I have always been and (unconsciously) who I will continue to be. The more we connect with the ideals and descriptions we apply to ourselves, the more potential there is for these to define us. This can then roll over to directing what we do and how we go about things. If we think of and relate to ourselves as 'clever', 'hard working', or alternatively 'stupid' or 'incompetent', this can result in quite a restricted sense of self. One result of this is that we can become increasingly inflexible in how we see and relate to the world. This can happen with respect to our chosen roles in life as well. I could describe myself to a new acquaintance by saying, 'I am a clinical psychologist' or 'I am someone who does clinical psychology for a job'. Can you see any difference in the potential for one of those descriptions to be somewhat more restricting?

With respect to this conceptualized self, a challenge for people who are moving on from burnout can come when you strongly relate not only to the self-descriptor but all that it might mean or be thought to entail. Thus, once in a career, you might feel that to be truly successful you have to comply rigidly with the expectations and requests from others and also those obligations that you personally feel are attached to the position.

To help balance out the unhelpful aspects of over-identifying with the conceptualized self, it can be beneficial to explore what is involved with flexible perspective-taking. This allows you to step back from the intimate involvement in a single view of life and encourages a perspective whereby you see yourself as an observer of experiences. This is in contrast to being a bound-up participant who has no control over what seem like almost predetermined events and behaviours. This stepping-back hopefully encourages a new perspective-taking and aims to bring about comfort with and flexibility around the story of 'Who I am, was and will be'. It can assist you to see that you have built up an image (or is that a mirage?) around yourself regarding what you do and how you need to act in the world. The problem with this self-image is that it is not fully fleshed out. Rather, it is more like a two-dimensional image printed on glass — one that can be seen clearly and gives the impression of completeness but in reality has no depth that can be worked with. As this imagery is experienced (and re-experienced) on such a regular basis (i.e. every time I reflect on who I am or go about doing something), it becomes a much-encountered guidebook for life. As a result, we tend to go to the well-thumbed chapters in this guidebook that have previously helped us in unfamiliar places and eventually forget to question whether the information is as relevant now as it once was.

An outdated guidebook

When I was doing my youthful travelling years ago, I came to rely upon a guidebook that most travellers had in their packs, from a series called *Let's Go*. This presented information about countries and regions within their borders. It was trusted by travellers as being a guide to the best sites, yummiest (and cheapest) food plus the local attractions. It helped guide my plans and the things I considered spending my rapidly vanishing funds upon. However, I eventually came to understand that the information was obtained by students travelling the previous year (or earlier) and that, with the best will possible, this information could not be seen as 'current'. But as I had already invested money in this weighty tome I continued to use it as my direction finder (yes, reader, this was before the time of smartphones and apps), even in the face of information and experiences that indicated it was not always particularly correct or useful. Time had simply moved on, but I and many others were still trying to apply the information from what had been (generally) a useful and trustworthy source. This meant that sometimes travellers anticipated things that were not deliverable or encountered situations that were different to what they were expecting.

I recall a scene at the Library of Celsus, at Ephesus in Turkey, surely one of the most amazing sights remaining from antiquity. Two young English-speaking women were remonstrating with the official at the site on admission costs. It was their contention that they should be charged a particular price based on the amount quoted in their guidebook. The hapless official patiently pointed to the sign, which clearly indicated the current admission prices, while the tenacious young women waved their copy of *Let's Go* and attempted to get the official to not only read the 'proof' but adjust his charges accordingly. Eventually, it became clear that the official was not going to budge and the travellers were faced with a choice: either pay what was advertised or miss out on entrance. These two young women took what they considered to be the moral high ground, refused to pay what was asked and left.

Rather than the above incident exemplifying a matter of principle, I would suggest it is a beautiful example of rigidly adhering to guidelines that are held to be true and then not adjusting or demonstrating any flexibility. This is despite clear indications that the approach is no longer valid or useful. In this case, holding onto the outdated guidelines came at a cost in terms of what these travellers encountered on their trip. If you have never seen this amazing building with all its memories and indicators of a past and glorious life, Google the 'Library of Celsus' and see just what these young people missed out on. I wonder how their day and their experiences might have been different if they had not relied on previously recorded information and their belief in this? How might their lives and memories have been enriched if they could have shifted a bit, been more flexible with their expectations and decision-making processes?

If we become too attached to who we are or have been — and therefore to what we feel we 'should' do — we risk repeating the same old actions and responses, even if they are proving to be less than useful. For you, as you try to navigate burnout, the risk is in tightly holding onto ways of behaving at work because this is 'who I am' ... or, rather, who you believe yourself to be. By learning to step back a little from the descriptors of ourselves and the image we relate to, we will be able to maintain a sense of 'who I am' but have greater flexibility.

A BETTER VIEW BY STEPPING BACK

Perhaps a key issue here is that that the view of ourselves may lack balance and perspective. This, of course, makes it hard to see things from any other angle or consider if decisions could have been taken differently and therefore led to another outcome. To do this requires some ability to psychologically distance ourselves from the story in our head. There can be some real positives from being able to de-automate this way of seeing ourselves and our relationship to our workplace or chosen career. What if we could develop an awareness that we are part of something yet are also able to watch and consider what is going on at the same time?

It is this issue of perspective that may be useful for people prone to burnout or not wanting to slip back into it. Of value is being aware that we have thoughts but they are not necessarily the totality of 'me', nor are they a call to action that cannot be ignored. Rather, coming to realize that we can have thoughts and feelings (e.g. 'I must work hard all the time', 'Every task needs to be perfect') but also observe them from a psychological distance without being directed by them, can be liberating. This freedom comes from not being completely attached to these thoughts and feelings or having an investment in them being enacted in a particular way, timeframe or with a certain outcome. As a result, 'good enough' may start to be an okay thing! By observing a thought and not automatically following it, we can start to prise apart this sense that 'I am what I think, which is me'. As a result, your sense of who you are can remain intact and healthy as it is not bound up in the content of the thought. The thoughts, ideas or plans are just that: thoughts, ideas and plans. Radical, huh?

Unfortunately, for consistently high performers there has often been a longstanding blurring of the boundaries between the self and the thinking. This can result in a drive to complete the ideas and plans, as they are experienced as being intimately associated with 'me' and 'who I am' — with associated risks for identity and mood. There is a melding of the person and the thoughts, which gets expressed via internal, demanding phrases such as 'I must always ...'. Note the lack of wriggle room with this internal language and the fact the individual has meshed with the thought. This is where the idea of stepping back (figuratively speaking) from the thinking process can assist. The approach can be conceived of as a way of monitoring or watching thoughts and processes as they come along, without being caught up with them or any associated feelings attached to these thoughts (e.g. 'I can't leave the office until everything is finished.'). The aim is to learn how to observe thoughts and ideas as if you are simply there to document what happens without intervening or promoting any behaviour (a bit like our previously mentioned naturalists in Africa simply observing the animals, but never intervening). By adopting this approach, you should be able to make and maintain the distinction between yourself and the thoughts/internal drivers you experience (e.g. to do a perfect job or to prove you are the most reliable person in the company).

You are not your thoughts

The important thing to realize is that the content of the idea is quite separate to who and what the person is. Just as a firefighter is not their uniform, you are not your thoughts. The professional firefighter retains knowledge about fires and safety issues at all times but they are not always part of the team required to put out fires. They have time out from that role and its demands and do not have to respond to the siren on their days off. A helpful approach would be for you to move into the observer or 'one-step-removed' role as and when needed — that is, to not feel obligated to always respond to or follow through on the demanding thoughts you have. This does not mean total detachment from every aspect of your life, but rather having the ability to identify and distinguish when unhelpful or pressuring thoughts are present and then to know how to slip into the observing role. If you do this, you can choose whether to follow the thoughts or an alternative path, which might make other options available. This can bring about an enhanced sense of control, one that is appropriate to the situation in front of you — rather than vainly trying to be totally in control of all things, at all times.

Why such an approach is important is that we can become trapped by cognitive processes that are built around the powerful rules and approaches learned early in life. To be fair, though, most people operate by general rules to some extent and these impact their decisions. During recent renovations, a friend's son entered the kitchen asking for a drink of water. However, the tap was out of action, so his dad suggested he go to the bathroom and get a drink from the tap there. The son's immediate response (accompanied by one of those priceless teenage facial expressions that clearly intimate Dad is insane) was 'Don't be so gross' and 'That's beyond wrong!'. My friend pointed out that his son used that tap and water to clean his teeth twice daily, and that the water for both areas came from the same source, but it made no difference. One tap was where drinking water came from and the other was apparently 'cleaning'-type water. Now, the son is a smart young man and not irretrievably trapped by age or convention, but I guess he had been socialized into seeing that you normally drink water and clean your teeth in different places, and never the twain shall meet!

With biased or strong cognitive processes directing things, there is a risk of becoming rigid in applying the 'rules' around how things should be done. If you are unable to be flexible at times of challenge and difficulty, you might retreat into your well-rehearsed coping behaviours. Invariably, this means pushing yourself harder, longer and more consistently, even in the face of evidence that this is no longer bearing fruit. I am suggesting that you might benefit from being able to disengage from these rules, cognitions and belief systems, as and when needed. One of the aims of changing this same style of responding is to ensure responses are not unduly restricted or narrowed by your internal language, beliefs and thoughts.

TO SUM UP

One of the best ways to respond to a changing environment is to be able to choose from options. This requires the ability to shift between these options and be open to choosing the one that best suits the current situation. One of the challenges for you is that you have tended to work within a narrowed perspective and may see only limited options (e.g. work harder, or make it perfect). Doing things on autopilot seems easier and more familiar but it might not allow you to consider variations or new approaches within the work environment.

Acceptance is not a dirty word, despite what your previous learning has led you to believe. It is not about giving in. It is about being open to options and experiences. It is also about working alongside and managing situations, not always trying to dominate them. You don't have to give up your control — in fact, you might find yourself feeling more in control if you account for the realities of a situation and acknowledge the feelings you are experiencing. This will allow you to see what is happening for you *here and now* and may help you to find the best approach for managing the current situation. A move from recycling old ways through to considering newer options is a big step forward, but one that will come about more readily if you drop the 'attack mode' and accommodate to the reality of the situation.

Developing a new perspective on your current work demands or wider life can help you to generate new, different or simply more options for responding. If you can step back from intense involvement with the situation, you will be able to observe more clearly what is happening or what is about to happen. It is perhaps time to consider letting go of the guidelines you have relied on for so long and trust that you can move forward without that well-worn roadmap of your life. Realize that you are infinitely more than the outline or description of what you have done before. You may just surprise yourself in terms of your creativity and novel problem-solving attributes. You are you, not just what you have previously done. Similarly, you are not the thoughts that you have, nor do they fully represent who you are or everything you are capable of!

A chance for change

To begin the shift towards flexibility in your life, you might like to embark on a positive process of reconfiguring your sense of self. This is not giving up on who you have been and it is especially not about seeking a completely new persona. Rather, it is about getting in touch with your personal values and letting them guide you with your choices and actions. If these things are aligned, you are more likely to head in a direction that will not only be satisfying but also more sustainable. The beauty of this approach is that you don't need to find someone new to become; you will notice that the attributes and building blocks are already present, and have been for a long time. The problem is that they have become out of balance and some important aspects of yourself may have slipped into the background. Now is the time to find out (or is that rediscover?) what these important aspects are. Reconfiguring is not the same as rebuilding; it is more about shuffling the positive traits and abilities that have always been present. These may have been, up to now, ordered and prioritized to facilitate achievements and high-level outcomes in your work life or to desperately try to keep your head above water in the workplace. However, much like a deck of cards, a bit of timely shuffling can often result in a much more useful hand to play in the next game ... or chapter in your life.

How might you like to live your life from here on in? Why not take some time to consider what it is that is truly important to you. This is about who and what you really want to be like, not what you think you *should* be like. If you can get in touch with these things that many people call 'values', they may help adjust those powerful schemas that have been driving you through life to this point. It is more about tapping into a purpose for your life rather than resetting a goal. Let's try to see if you can identify what you really want from, and within, key domains in your life.

TRY THIS

Set out below are some key areas, or domains, of life. Choose one or more that is relevant to you and your busy existence to this point. Then, take a pen and paper and under your chosen heading/s, list the values you would like to demonstrate daily and live by — a couple of examples are provided to start you off. Remember, values are about the personal qualities you would like to exhibit in each domain (rather than goals such as to be rich or to be the boss).

Domain	Value/s
Work	e.g. To be proud of my performance but not let this dominate my life
Physical activity	
Family	e.g. To be available for my kids and share time in the evenings
Arts/hobbies	

> Once you have completed this, try to consider what your life might be like when you live according to these important aspects. This can lead you to exploring what you might need to change in your life to begin balancing things out.
>
> Also, how about choosing one of these values each day and then trying to breathe some life into it by expressing it, living by it or just trying to show this aspect to someone/the world? Start small, get a feel for it and then try to make these a part of how you wish your life to proceed going forward.

Another question to explore at this point is whether it might be okay to consider looking at things from a different perspective. Is it okay to be a bit kinder to yourself when you encounter a challenging situation? Rather than pushing on with over-familiar approaches to life that don't permit flexibility, maybe it is time to pull back and re-identify those things that are actually important for you. Shifting away from the focus on setting goals may permit you to develop a better balance between those should-dos and want-to-dos. When was the last time you actually accounted for the personally important things rather than responding with the externally demanded or expected behaviours? This is not about becoming self-indulgent. Rather, it is about finding some degree of middle ground. No, this is not shirking or giving up; this is standing back, looking at all the options and considering what *you choose* to do here, in this situation, at this time but also as you go forward and reclaim your world, following the experience of burnout.

TRY THIS

If you are particularly keen, this strategy can help you begin the process of learning to view things from another perspective. If you can get the feel of how to do this, you might be able to shift to another, more helpful view on any given situation. You can then see if it brings up any options for responding that you had not previously considered. It may also permit you to see that you don't have to beat up on yourself because things were not 'perfect'.

Let's try some visualization. All you will need for this exercise is a pen, some paper and your imagination. Imagine that you are an interviewer for a television science show. You are presenting a show on colour blindness and you are going to interview a person who is colour blind. Your task is to get across to the audience just what it is like to live with colour blindness, how it impacts a person's life, and to give a feel for what it might be like to experience this. Prior to starting the visualization, take a few minutes to think about what questions you'd like to ask the 'interviewee' and write them down on your sheet of paper. Remember, you are trying to help people gain an understanding of life from the interviewee's point of view. Therefore, try to use open, 'wondering' questions that will help you and others understand something you have not personally experienced and may not have ever considered. Think about what your viewers need to hear so that they can make sense of and work with this new knowledge.

Now that you have your questions, settle back in a comfortable, quiet place with no distractions. Relax into

> your chair, close your eyes and see yourself on the set of a television program. Visualize all the detail of the surroundings, as if you are really in a TV studio. Once you can see the scene and your interviewee, engage them in conversation and lead into the questions you have prepared. This is where the perspective-taking aspect comes in — allow this person to answer your questions in as much detail as they want. Yes, it is you 'putting words in their mouth' and that is the whole point of the exercise. If 'they' can answer the questions in a way that represents life with colour blindness, you are actually shifting from your perspective to that of another.
>
> Practise this a few times and then try using this new ability of considering another perspective the next time you encounter a challenging situation. This may allow you to step aside from your usual response set and consider something new or different. This might be in terms of how you see the problem or situation, what you can do about it and then how you talk to yourself about it.

This chapter is not trying to suggest that it is easy to adapt, to accommodate and to become more flexible. It takes time to develop the necessary skills and they cannot always be put into place immediately to alter the direction of events or your response to them. To reinforce this point, I offer the following observation. My wife and I were returning from several weeks travelling through countries with a very casual standard of dress. On the final leg of the flight home, we entered the plane's cabin only to be directed to palatial-looking seats in business class. The elusive and oft-dreamed-about upgrade had finally happened. However, we were clothed like dishevelled bohemians and looking as if we would be more at home in a beach hut. Talk about negative cognitions and strong emotions racing in; uncomfortable doesn't even begin to cover this! No matter how I tried, I found it difficult to settle back into the luxurious environment and enjoy the gratis goodies. I also recall struggling to figure out how to use the entertainment system but could not bring myself to ask for assistance, as this would surely prove to the staff that I did not usually fly business class. So, there I was, sitting in luxury and completely unable to enjoy the experience as my head was full of negative talk and my gut was consumed with angst around being identified as a fraud. Darwin would be horrified at my inability to size up the environment, modify my actions and fit in!

10.

PLOTTING A (FUTURE) LIFE COURSE AMIDST AND BEYOND BURNOUT

Throughout this book, you will have become acquainted with the effects of living with burnout. Your struggles with this condition may well have stymied progress in areas of life that have been important to you. However, much of this perhaps has not been news to you; the chances are that you were attracted to this book because you have been living the reality of having burnout and its impact on your life's journey.

Hopefully, after working your way to this point of the book, you have become more confident that something can (and should) be done about burnout and its effects on you. By gaining an awareness of the practical strategies in the book, you will be better placed to work with the effects of burnout as they arise or continue to be present. This will open up the chances of you having a renewed perspective on what is in front of you, with less threat being apparent and more management options coming to the fore. Remember, though, you will never be able to completely avoid or hide from the potential for burnout. It is a part of being human in a big, complex and increasingly demanding world. Using — and continuing to use — your new skills is going to be important now. Please don't leave the information and management strategies as 'theory' or 'understanding'. Rather, relate to these important aspects as practical and experiential approaches you can use to take you forward in a more adaptive and confident manner. In that vein, this chapter is going to highlight the merit in having some other/new purpose in your life. For any number of reasons, work has taken that role up until now. The aim is to help you to reset your course after a challenging time and trust yourself to reinvigorate your capabilities. Burnout and the associated challenges may have influenced your life but, from now on, they do not need to define it!

Remember, there is a narrowing of perspective that comes along with your struggle with burnout and the feelings of being overwhelmed. This means you might not see alternatives and you can miss out on potentially positive outcomes and shifts within your world. Why? Because — due to ongoing pressure and demands within the workplace— you have become attuned to what can, and seemingly will, go wrong. It is this (understandable) narrow lens on life and your circumstances that can hold you back from renewed achievement and personal growth.

How you relate to and therefore experience events will have direct effects on your confidence in whether you can navigate your way through difficulties. If you can become more comfortable with knowing there is a way through burnout, you may be able to ignite the desire to do, be and achieve. What if you can learn from these challenges and use that knowledge or new perspective to grow as a person?

PURPOSE: BUZZ WORD OR IMPORTANT CONCEPT?

The experience of burnout can leave you struggling with day-to-day practical things, the issue of what your next job might look like, or more philosophical questions such as where you are headed in life. These struggles and confusion can feel normal after becoming run down and overwhelmed by burnout. However, if you can develop an understanding of what is important to you, and resolve to make this happen, then you may be on course to have a more meaningful and fulfilling future. Knowing where you want to head and what it is that you are looking for can reduce or remove the dread and negative anticipation about your future life. This can shrink the uncertainty to a more manageable size. A problem with negative anticipation is that it teaches you that things unknown must be bad or threatening. Your brain takes you to that perspective like moths racing towards a light source. Over time, you automatically and unquestioningly return to that view of things being bad, just like our paraphyletic friends keep returning to the porch light when you turn it on each night. This leaves you with a sense that there is nothing out there except threat and trouble. Not a happy view of the world, is it?

I want to reinforce that it will be helpful to unlearn this automatic appraisal process. This is so there might be room for something kinder and more interesting in your future. If you have a sense of some purpose in life, you should be able to work your way through what life throws at you. Think about some of the new skills and approaches you have just learned. Use them as a lens to look at options ahead of you. As a part of this, you can begin to take what ACT terms 'committed action', in service of attaining the goal/s and direction you have identified.

Note the use of the word 'action', which is a doing word — not a waiting word. It speaks to you taking some degree of control and moving purposefully towards a valued place in your life. One that may well be quite different, in terms of role, structure and expectations. This is where you are no longer held hostage by external demands and begin to see positive and fulfilling things ahead of you. Choosing to explore options and being open to the positive aspects of life will ensure that your brain begins to get some balance instead of being weighted towards all the negatives that burnout has been training you to see. This is about putting you back in the centre of your own life. The place where you are standing up and taking responsibility to bring things to fruition.

Purpose can be on a big scale and relate to your life's direction or it can be about what you want to get out of each day. There is no need to equate purpose and meaning to only deep philosophical issues or life-altering experiences. It is possible to bring purpose to your life by having a connection to your garden, your artwork, your role as a parent or being part of a community group. This awareness and understanding can bring some clarity of focus on what it is that you need to be doing — at whatever level — to meet your purpose. The result can be seen in terms of achievement but also in terms of satisfaction and personal control. These are important personal aspects that have probably been missing because of your experience with burnout.

One of the key elements to establishing some purpose in life is to be working towards something. This relates to some of the skills that we know you have from your work life — goal setting and planning. If you have them in your repertoire, you can be building toward a new and healthier purpose. None of this is just theory, of course; the planning and goal setting must be supported by action — the 'doing' part I mentioned above. This can be around achieving a daily task or it can be related to a long-held desire or bucket list item.

Living a life that has purpose to it is important. This involves knowing and feeling that there is something you want to do and stand for. If you see your life as having purpose, you have at your disposal a 'touchstone' that can help you nudge towards the uncertainty and see that life ahead of you (post-burnout) does not need to be empty. Viktor Frankl, in his powerful work *Man's Search for Meaning*, noted that it is not possible to control everything that happens to you in life. Despite this, he asserts that you do have the ability to choose what you feel and do in the face of events. This brings us back to that notion of a personal 'touchstone', whereby you are connected to your values and what you identify as a purpose for your life. These aspects can act as guides to your decisions when faced with repeated demands. You will not always have to struggle with burnout, although it may often feel like that. Where you get to will develop from how you make sense of situations, how you account for your values plus your sense of purpose.

Having a purpose is an ingredient to living a life that is fulfilling. If you can identify some purpose, you will be pulled towards the direction you want to head because there is a tight fit with your values. However, identifying this purpose is a process; it is not something that usually appears in a dream or a sudden bout of inspiration. It is built on the basis of your values and notions of how you would like your life to be. These values will operate as a form of scaffolding to develop the direction you want to go, as they will incorporate what is central to you. Of course, this is not a simple set-and-forget process. You may find that these factors benefit from fine tuning, adjustments and occasionally a rebuild along the way. That is acceptable and usual. There are always those annoying, but well put together individuals who 'just know' what their purpose is. For most of us there is a degree of trial and error but, most importantly, some refinement as we progress.

Consider identifying and developing some purpose in your life as a way to get out of the starting blocks (post-burnout). This comes from doing personally relevant, useful, enjoyable, rewarding or values-congruent activities (each is valid). By understanding yourself and what is important to you, a sense of purpose is more likely to be developed. If you know your purpose, you can begin to gain a sense of control over what is happening and where things are going. This will help set your focus and guide your actions and behaviours. This doesn't have to be about aiming for a Nobel Prize. It can be about helping (family, friends, community), doing (working towards your important targets at home or in general life) or planning for a potentially new career path. In some ways, this is a voyage of discovery, a way to get to know yourself better, and then making choices that fit with who you see yourself to be. It is also about taking ownership of your life, by bringing into existence things that are going to bring positivity into your world. This is the active part of this process, where you deliberately make things happen and work to breathe life into them. What follows from this is the experience of meaning within your life, an associated increase in self-confidence and enhanced abilities to tolerate uncertainty and disruptions to your world. It will help you cope with setbacks and let you see there is more to you than you realized, which will aid with the development of personal resilience.

IKIGAI: WHY YOU GET UP EACH DAY

For a refreshing take on having meaning in life, let's consider the Japanese approach of ikigai. This is a word that encompasses your reason for doing things. It is felt and experienced in such a way that a person knows they can move forward in a positive and active manner. Ikigai is about having purpose flow from this approach to life.

Developing such a relationship to life (i.e. to have ikigai) can set you up to have a healthier, more fulfilling life. That, in itself, must surely be refreshing after the experience of burnout. It also provides you with a way of interacting with life that brings in important approaches and actions. Neuroscientist and writer Ken Mogi describes ikigai as being about discovering, defining and appreciating life's pleasures that have meaning for the individual. This can be so important after having your personal life disrupted or even hijacked by burnout. He goes on to talk about ikigai as the reason to get up each morning and as giving you motivation for living your life.

One of the central pillars of ikigai is about embracing and actively living the notion of operating within the present. This is something that might have slipped away as you spent time worrying about the outcomes of tasks, meetings and work relationships. As a part of this new approach, there is an attention to detail and a grasping of what is happening in front of you, and not spending time and energy on future issues. The latter has probably been characterized by the negative anticipation and worry built up within a life affected by burnout, which then undermined your sense of control. Operating within this new realm is part and parcel of having ikigai in your life. It fits well with approaching life and activities in a way that demonstrates a commitment to achieving, but in a positive, manageable and respectful way. This is very different to the slavish following of high standards and pushing to complete tasks that you have experienced for so long now. Ikigai acknowledges that life offers up things and you do not often get a choice about what is given to you. However, accepting this reality and looking at what you can do within the situation will help to take you forward. Consider your approach to life as an adaptive process, whereby you are guided by the fundamental aspects of your own ikigai, despite what things seem like in front of you. Of relevance to us is the idea that operating with your ikigai as a guide permits you to engage with whatever is presented to you. It means that you don't have to worry excessively about what is coming or what you think the situation should be. Following your ikigai will assist you to be more consistent in life and able to bounce back if you encounter difficulties. Here we are talking about resilience — more to come on that soon. The workplace and general life in a complex world can be daunting. However, living your ikigai will help you to weather those challenges and cope with the uncertainty, instead of heading down that rabbit hole of being unsure and overwhelmed.

A fundamental aspect of ikigai is to be comfortable in your own skin: accepting yourself as you are and not as you feel you must be. The latter can be a source of strife and dissatisfaction due to the struggle with an idealized sense of self. This is often what has developed over time and within the context of a demanding and outcome-oriented employment situation. What your ikigai looks like and what it involves will be an individual thing; it is not an off-the-rack experience. However, if you can grasp what yours involves and how it operates, you have a better chance of being settled and happy. If you are doing and living your ikigai by staying active via low-intensity exercise, surrounding yourself with good friends, connecting with nature, being grateful, living in the moment and mindfully participating in rewarding tasks, you will be in a far better place to work through the pressures of challenging situations. The same goes for the bigger issues such as your career or life's direction.

The literal meaning of ikigai is to have a reason to get up each day and then do things. The things you do might be important, interesting, fun or functional. They do not have to be purely achievement- and performance-oriented. It is also about accepting that your life and the world you inhabit are not perfect and there is no handbook that prepares you for every situation you will encounter. The positive attitude that flows from being aware of your ikigai can foster a sense of optimism that will help you to see potential and opportunity in what previously may have seemed like negative or overwhelming situations. On the island of Okinawa there is a strong connection to ikigai and it is suggested that having this is an important aspect of why the island's inhabitants live so long and report very low levels of stress.

Ikigai flows on to purpose and this can be about your purpose for each day. It does not have to be about goals, targets and rising through the corporate ranks. Ikigai can help to direct your energy and effort. In their book *Ikigai: The Japanese secret to a long and happy life*, authors Garcia and Miralles note that the Okinawans go about their functioning in a settled and relaxed manner, where there is no emphasis on rushing. There may well be something in this approach that assists people to achieve, feel good about themselves and meet challenges (including unexpected ones). These authors suggest that, after you have identified your ikigai, following its course and growing it on a daily basis will bring meaning to your life. They further suggest that, once you have some purpose in your life, you will approach all that you do in a manner that maximizes your potential to cope with demands and activities.

MEANING IN LIFE

Living a life that has meaning to it is important. This is about knowing and feeling that there is something you want to do and stand for. Viktor Frankl offers that our task is to see our own life as being meaningful, no matter what we are faced with. (Is it truly about working hard to the exclusion of all else?)

Each of us does have some choice. Frankl talks about the individual being challenged to change themselves when the situation is not clear or solvable. He mentions that your attitude towards the situation is within your power to change. Here, he is talking about adopting an approach that builds from the meaning you find in your life and altering your attitude to one that brings forth helpful and adaptive responses. This is consistent with what you have been learning in this book. If you struggle with feeling powerless, you tend to see what might go wrong and how difficult things are. Having a sense of meaning that emanates from a place of problem-solving and adaptation is helpful to tap into. It will also shift you and your perspective away from the identification of threat and what seems like an inability to bring about change. You do not always have to struggle with what seems like hopelessness, although it may often feel like that. You have the choice (as well as chances) to make change happen. Where you get to might be more related to how you make sense of the situation, how you account for your values and your own sense of meaning, than the lack of a clear pathway ahead of you.

As we have seen from exploring ikigai, having a purpose is an ingredient for living a fulfilled life, and therefore brings meaning to your world. We are talking about following, participating in, navigating alongside or simply being guided by this purpose. By doing this you will also be on a voyage of discovery, one whereby you can identify and acknowledge your attributes or strengths. These will help you to shape your purpose along the journey, so that it is something you can relate to and feel okay striving for. It shouldn't be dominating or directing you. Rather, if you can identify a purpose you will be pulled towards the direction you are wanting to head.

To bring this purpose to fruition is a process built on a basis of your values and notions of how you would like your life to be. These values will operate as a form of scaffolding to develop the direction you want to go, as they will incorporate what is central to you.

Identifying and developing some meaning in your life is a way to get you out moving, possibly in a new direction, particularly if you have lived the draining and often overwhelming sequelae from burnout. We all need to make some sense of our lives and this will flow through to the goals we set and directions we choose. Having a purpose will help set your focus and guide your actions and behaviours. This is a way to get to know yourself better and then make choices that fit with who you see yourself to be. It is also about taking ownership of your life, by bringing positivity into existence.

TRY THIS

This exercise brings together many aspects we have just been talking about. It is a psychologically safe way of exploring values, meaning and purpose, in relation to the person you would like to show up as, following the experience of burnout. I'm going to ask you to use your imagination to 'build' an avatar of the future self you would like to be.

If you have played video/online games, you will be familiar with the term 'avatar'. Essentially, an avatar is a graphical representation of yourself in another world or dimension (i.e. the environment of the game). In this exercise, your avatar will embody the skills, abilities, strengths, morals, behaviours and even wardrobe that you consider to be a valid approximation of you.

Consider what attributes you would like to see this avatar demonstrating as they go about life, outside of the smothering grip of burnout. Try to be a little creative with this task, so that it doesn't become an intellectual exercise alone. You can certainly make a list of key words but you can also use images, drawings and figures to represent you and the attributes you wish to be living by and with. Some of my clients have drawn a picture of themselves and then framed this with words, definitions, arrows, boxes — the only limit is your imagination.

Your avatar will be the embodiment of your knowledge, skills and understanding in relation to participating in a post-burnout future. Consider some of the following as guides for what to include:

- Your values, e.g. caring for yourself
- Desirable attributes, e.g. being flexible with your perspective
- Key strengths, e.g. assertiveness
- Physical activities you might like to do, e.g. walking for fitness

- Interpersonal skills, e.g. communicating clearly and respectfully
- Having a purpose, e.g. to be present for family and friends
- Meaning.

See this avatar as a model and a map for who you would like to be and how you would like to act in your new relationship to your life and all its dimensions ... not just work. As with any computer game, you can come back to your avatar and update, refresh or extend it, based on new perspectives, interests or desires. See this as a living document that represents the new you, as you move forward with your life.

11.

BUILDING FOR THE FUTURE, DESPITE THE UNCERTAINTY OF BURNOUT

Living with burnout can be difficult and trying. As we have seen, it can trip us up across many areas of our lives. Hopefully, though, you are starting to realize there are things that can be done to dampen the effects of burnout and what it does to your body and mind. Alongside the strategies and approaches you have learned from this book, it is important to be aware that burnout can remain a vulnerability of yours. This is not a negative message. It is acknowledgement that, in life, each of us is going to face challenging things, sometimes repeatedly, and we are better off if we can find ways to deal with them. Burnout brings along with it many challenges — to our confidence, sense of self and even our future direction in life. A lot of this goes unnoticed until it has announced its presence and then it often feels too late. However, living with burnout is a bit like inviting your friend on a road trip in your small car, only to find, when you pull up at their house to pick them up, they keep bringing out bag after bag of luggage. Instead of yelling at them or calling the trip off, you need to find ways to pack the bags so things aren't too uncomfortable for you, they don't impede your vision and they don't inhibit your experience of the journey. Not ideal, but at least you are able to continue on your way, with some adjustments and adaptations.

RESILIENCE: BURNOUT'S NEMESIS

Let's now look at resilience and explore why it is relevant to working alongside burnout and reclaiming (or extending) your sense of control. The place to start is with the acknowledgement that burnout is already present or looming large in your world. It is not an unfair visitation from the gods. Rather, it is an outcome of a challenging nexus between workplace conditions and aspects of how you operate (e.g. powerful schemas). Next is exploring your relationship with and attitude towards burnout. The goal is to work with this issue, as you are better off approaching it from a place of understanding and with a sense that you can work your way through it.

So, what are we talking about with this resilience thing? In essence, it is about being able to recover from or find ways to adapt positively to unpleasant situations or change. What it is not, is about being tough, strong and staunch. It is also not about rolling over and feeling defeated by burnout and all that that brings with it. Humans sit somewhere on a continuum in terms of how resilient they are. (Ever noticed how psychologists see just about everything as being on a continuum? Well, it isn't a cop-out or sugary explanation. It highlights that most of life is not an either/or issue.) With resilience, you are not born with a full loading that means you will cope better than everyone else. Similarly, it is not true that you will never be able to cope with adversity or challenges. The truth is that we need to encounter some adversity to challenge ourselves, make some gains and then become more confident about managing things. This helps us to see that we can cope and that it is possible to carry on with life, despite the challenges along the way. The good news is that resilience can be seen as a range of skills that everyone can learn and develop. This will enable you to more confidently handle any future challenges associated with burnout and its impact on your life.

One of the key aspects of resilient people is that they see a central role for themselves in bringing about their accomplishments. They also appear to be in tune with what is happening for them internally (e.g. regarding their thoughts, feelings and the processing of these). Being able to manage these dimensions gives you an advantage when approaching challenging situations and events. The skills presented within the earlier chapters will assist you to regulate your emotional states and responses, which fits beautifully with developing resilience. This reinforces the earlier suggestions around practising and honing the management skills for difficulties associated with burnout. Having a powerful emotional response can key you into what can go wrong. Conversely, being able to regulate your emotions can set you up to see ways through and to consider potential, such as a chance to learn something beneficial. Leveraging the skills you have been presented with so far, you will be able to increase your chances of attaining positive outcomes in the face of burnout.

Another aspect of importance to our aim of managing the effects of burnout is the adaptable nature of resilient people. This is in terms of their psychological perspective and the flexibility they bring with them to any situation. By shifting your perspective and being open to alternatives, you are better able to identify solutions and potential ways around the unhelpful thoughts and feelings that come with burnout. Resilient people are like that classic eastern description of the bamboo versus the willow: the former will bend and shift with the wind, whilst the latter will stand firm and not budge an inch. Unfortunately, the willow ends up taking the full force of the wind and risks breaking. Our bamboo, however, will bend and then bounce back to its original position — maintaining its core features and potential to grow. A resilient person maintains this openness to ideas and options, with a focus on finding an outcome that works for what they are faced with.

By developing a more optimistic approach to considering what is possible in the face of unknowns, you will also be building your resilience. This is added to by having an approach that considers options and sees positives — not in a delusional sense, but a realistic one. Such optimism can come from shifting the closed and rigid perspective to one where you actively look for ways to settle or ameliorate the effects of burnout. We have talked about using your energy to work with things that you can influence, and not worry about and spend precious time on things that are beyond your current abilities. This is channelling the realistic, practical aspect of your nature as well, by problem-solving the challenge in front of you.

Hopefully you can see that the approaches we have explored in the book will build your confidence to do things, in the face of (and after) burnout. This confidence in yourself and your capabilities is another hallmark of the resilient individual. However, if things are tough and don't seem easily sorted or made sense of, don't beat yourself up. Be forgiving and kind to yourself. Not having things work out just as you want does not mean you are inadequate or that burnout has defeated you. If you can cut yourself some slack and don't let that harsh internal critic loose, you may just find that you have more energy to come back to the challenge, perhaps with a renewed perspective.

WHAT'S SO GREAT ABOUT BEING RESILIENT?

Resilience can help you to cope with challenges and respond in a flexible, adaptive manner. Perhaps more importantly, being resilient means you are more likely to pick yourself up after a disappointment or setback and begin to look for options to keep moving forward. Research identifies that resilient people are better able to cope with the challenges of life. This is because they have the ability to move on from difficulties. Part of this is the attitude of getting back on course after encountering a setback. It doesn't necessarily mean they are not affected by tough situations. Rather, it is about knowing they can make their way back from adversity. Something of relevance to our discussion is that enhanced resilience helps you to adapt to and work alongside the symptoms and effects of burnout. This is because resilient people are comfortable being in the presence of their emotions, as opposed to fighting them or running from them. They also understand that they have skills and personal resources that can assist them to get through a challenging time. It is helpful to remember that resilience is built up from encountering challenges, not from being in a safe and comfortable life all the time. With the lived experience of working through difficult situations, you will have a personal narrative that is centred around being able to handle things that life throws at you. This knowledge and self-belief are key to moving forward in times of difficulty.

Perhaps one of the important things about being resilient is that it allows you to consciously choose how you want to respond to a dilemma. The practical nature within such people can let them key into what is happening in front of them, at that moment. This is about working with what you have, as opposed to what you want things to be. It is also about not being distracted by the emotional responses that might sway their choice of action.

The latter can see you grasp at solutions and respond in ways that may not be the most helpful, such as moving away from things that seem unpleasant or scary. This involves having a mindful approach to burnout, whereby the resilient person can accept that there is burnout present (not hope for it to be otherwise) and then work with what comes up. So, how you go about interacting with these experiences and what you do in the face of such situations can have implications for your general life and wellbeing. If you can feel confident in yourself to approach the challenges (physical and emotional), you will be able to access the skills and management options within you.

There will, of course, be difficulties, even when you are confident in what you bring to a situation. However, if you have kept your resilience tanked up, you will be able to pick yourself up more easily and then reset your course in life. By tapping into your inner strengths and skills, you will be able to move forward without being overrun by feelings of inadequacy or discouragement. This is important. As we have seen, being chased down by burnout can set you up to experience strong negative emotions and feelings of being overwhelmed, which can get you to hit pause or even feel like giving in. Perhaps one of the biggest advantages of resilience is that you don't need to worry so much about what is about to appear in your world, because you will have confidence in yourself and your problem-solving abilities. This will help to keep you grounded and not fearful of the unknowns that can lead to us feeling overwhelmed.

This, of course, is not about pretending or fooling yourself that you can control everything. It is about knowing you can target your focus onto the here and now and look for what you can influence. This will be both emotionally and physically energy saving, as you don't spiral into the worry zone and dwell on the uncertainty and potential costs that appear to be in front of you. By doing this, you are more likely to see the creative, the potential and the opportunities that could be ahead of you. Unfortunately, struggling with all that is involved with burnout and being overwhelmed by it can steal these gains from you — even before you get a chance to try them out! When you see nothing but heartache and problems in your life, your enjoyment and sense of being fulfilled will be reduced or perhaps elusive. This can, unfortunately, reinforce to you that life is narrow and lacking in future meaningful achievements.

WHAT DOES A RESILIENT PERSON LOOK AND ACT LIKE?

Although we all have a level of resilience, some people are more developed along this continuum than others. It is about being adaptive when things are unclear or threatening. We are not equally resilient in all domains of our lives, but it is fair to say that, if you have strengthened your resilience muscles, you are more likely to use them in whatever setting challenges you.

A resilient person would demonstrate some or many of the following:
- Has an awareness that a person's ability to control things has its limits; they will use their energy on issues that they can influence.
- Values connections with other people and is comfortable about seeking help.
- Relates to change and challenge as an opportunity, as opposed to something to be fearful of.
- Has a well-established and solid sense of self-efficacy.

- Is able to work with changes to their emotional state and not be overrun by strong emotions.
- Doesn't rush into things or expect outcomes to be quickly obtained.
- Accepts that life is not straightforward and will involve challenges.
- Maintains a positive (but not unrealistic) perspective on life and in the face of difficulties.
- Is confident within themselves and holds a positive sense of who they are.
- Has the ability to plan in a way that is realistic, and can implement those plans.
- Has strengths related to problem-solving and knows how to apply these skills across different domains.
- Maintains a perspective on life that sees setbacks as time limited and not set in concrete.
- Sees challenges (and uncertainty) as opportunities for development and as having potential.
- Tend not to take it personally when bad stuff happens or see themselves as victims of the situation.
- Seems to have what is termed a growth mindset — this incorporates being open to change and looking at how they might adapt to what is facing them.
- Has an awareness of personal values and the positive role they play in life planning.

A chance for change

The above section outlines core attributes of a resilient person. It might be interesting (and helpful) to reflect on what sort of fit you feel there is for you. Remember, it's not that people are resilient or not resilient. You will probably find that you demonstrate and live by some, or perhaps many, of the above attributes. Additionally, some of these will be strengths that you have while others are either absent or present in a minor way. By getting a feel for your current level of each attribute, you will be able to see which skills you could enhance, or develop, to build up your resilience.

Take a pen and piece of paper and then look again at the list of attributes above. For each one, consider honestly where you are feel you are at with living and applying each attribute. Rate each skill as: A) = not me at all; B) = present, but I could enhance this/ learn how to apply it more or C) = A big part of who I am and how I operate, and write your answer down. You should end up with sixteen letters. Now answer the following questions:

- What is your ratio of A and B ratings to C?
- What might this mean for you and your relationship to burnout and its effects?
- Thinking about what you have read in this book, how might you be able to work on or build up each of those A and B ratings?
- How many C ratings do you have? Congratulations on having these excellent attributes in your life. Just make sure you don't let them become rusty from disuse. Also, how about building up the A and B ratings to support these great skills you are already employing? What might this mean for you?

Building for the future, despite the uncertainty of burnout

Being resilient can help you respond more effectively to the effects of burnout. Burnout is a thing and bad things do happen. However, if you are confident in yourself and your management strategies, you will be able to bounce back from the difficulties that developing burnout can bring. Part of being a resilient person is accepting that nobody's life is always smooth sailing and predictable. Having the attitude that nobody should expect things to be perfect is protective against changes to your mood and confidence.

Being able to handle the unexpected outcomes and challenges from burnout is partly about knowing the difference between what you feel you should control and what you can actually influence.

The uncertainty associated with burnout promotes the identification of threats and there are a lot of negative feelings that come along with these. Your brain struggles to differentiate a big threat from a little one and a real one from a perceived one. Working through these distinctions will help your resilience to these challenges.

It is you that affects your ability to cope and get through challenging situations. If you are resilient, you will know this within yourself and that can open up possibilities for the future.

BECOMING MORE RESILIENT

If you can enhance your resilience, you are less likely to be pulled into that space where things feel overwhelming and beyond you. Adaptation in the face of an apparently threatening situation will bring forth that positive, coping-oriented and open mindset that will help you build on your strengths. Ways to do this can include:

- Notice the positives and look for the potential in situations — not just what seems obvious or apparent.
- Tell yourself that not knowing everything is normal and okay.
- Decide to work through things by using your problem-solving skills. Realize that not succeeding first time around is *not* the same as failure.
- Monitor your reactions to difficult situations. Are they sorting the situation out and assisting you or are they undermining things and keeping you stuck?
- Work on your decision-making skills.
- Have the belief that you can get through the threats and uncertainty associated with burnout. (This comes from trying and adapting your approaches.)
- Be active with choices around what you will focus on — the threat and what might go wrong, or the potential for the future and your ability to deal with things?
- Notice what you can do, what skills you have; not what you don't have or can't do.
- Check in deliberately with your thoughts and behaviours — critique them. Are they helping you deal with situations? If not, replace them with more helpful ones.
- Realize that resilience is about coping with adversity and unfamiliarity as it appears — not managing life at its best.
- Accept that not all outcomes are fantastic or immediately successful, and that coping has a wide definition. Hold back on the desire for perfection and, especially, hold off on the self-criticism.

- Be open and curious, just like you were as a child, or as if you are a beginner in ballet or karate class.
- Learn to regulate your emotions and associated responses. Enhancing this ability will help build your resilience by letting you become comfortable with the presence of emotions and understanding that they do not need to control you or your actions.
- Be aware of what you have within you — your strengths and abilities — so you can play to and with these.
- Don't be the one who stops or gets paralyzed. Be the one who actively chooses and decides.

TO SUM UP

Burnout is real and it can be debilitating. You can't always tell when you are going to bump into it but if you have skills (and confidence in yourself), you are on the way to more effectively working with it when it shows up.

Resilience is not a fixed attribute. It is about skills and being able, and willing, to implement them. These skills can be learned and developed.

Being resilient doesn't mean that burnout won't affect you. However, it does mean you will be better placed to deal with it and the effects won't be so powerful or long lasting on you.

This book has provided you with an array of skills to manage burnout and they are also relevant for building your resilience. This aspect of yourself will then help you to cope with burnout when you come across it. Lovely and circular, in a positive way!

The better you get with these skills, the easier you will find it to deal with the stress of burnout in your life. More particularly, you will bounce back quicker if/when it does visit your world.

Resilience is not about being tough or just enduring. It is an approach to life that helps you notice what is relevant. It can also prevent you from heading down a rabbit hole associated with strong emotions and poor decisions. You can assist this by focusing on the aspects that you can influence and staying in the present moment, which will allow more effective problem-solving. Worrying about the future and what might happen destabilizes you.

At the end of the day, resilience is a skill set that can be developed. The approaches within this skill set will serve you well in terms of building your tolerance to the challenging aspects of burnout. By building these skills and continuing to finetune them, you are giving yourself a better chance to work with the unknowns in life and forge a meaningful pathway for yourself.

12.

THE PARTNER'S JOURNEY (OR THE CANARY IN THE COALMINE)

Throughout the book I have been concentrating on ways of identifying and understanding what happens to, for and within the person who has experienced burnout. However, alongside this person there is often a travel-weary partner who has been there for a journey that they didn't perhaps always comprehend. These good folk have seen repeating patterns of behaviour and realized these were potentially problematic but perhaps did not know what they could do to help or bring about some change.

There is usually a rather special dance that develops between the driven or A/N individual and their partner. Here we are talking about the spouse/partner who has waited patiently at home as the time of the concert draws ever near, or watched as the dinner they cooked spoils in the oven due to their special person not arriving home as expected. These people tend to have shown exceptional tolerance and patience as they (repeatedly) hear the promises to the kids about an upcoming outing, while knowing full well that something else may take precedence.

Many of these partners have known in their heart of hearts that the extent of the behaviours they have witnessed and tolerated is not 'usual'. Often, they have wondered why their special person has to be so dedicated and focused upon achieving goal after goal or meeting the demands of the workplace. The partner has essentially been engaged in this journey at multiple levels. On the one hand they have been an observer, one who has been a step removed from the behaviour but nonetheless able to view what is happening... and may well continue to happen. The partner is often conflicted within this role. For the most part, they want to support their special person with each endeavour and hope that they reach their goals and dreams, and perform in a way that satisfies their employer. However, they also spend a fair chunk of their time filling in the gaps and explaining to children, family and friends why the whole family can't make it to a particular occasion. Anything sounding familiar so far?

Rebecca is a capable professional who has come to understand that her husband embodies many characteristics of a driven personality. He has been involved with his own business for a number of years and this has been taking ever-increasing amounts of his time and energy. Recently, the importance of this venture has become a focal point for certain personality characteristics that we have been reading about. This has resulted in Rebecca's husband spending increasing amounts of time on work-related issues as well as being at the workplace for longer hours, and Rebecca has found that there is less time for them as a couple. She has also noticed that her husband's stress levels have been much higher and that he finds it hard to wind down from the demands of the expanding enterprise. Additionally, he is increasingly experienced as 'grumpy', more often tired and less attentive, plus he is experiencing increasingly disturbed sleep patterns. Another aspect of note is that the work plans and issues tend to dominate all conversations between the couple.

Despite Rebecca being an insightful and caring person, she is struggling to help her husband see the negative impact upon him of working so intensely, over such a long period. She is also starting to find herself alone in a relationship, which she can now articulate is not really what she signed up for in the marriage.

It is not uncommon to hear stories similar to Rebecca's when you work with people who live alongside someone with burnout. Over the years, I have seen some strong similarities between the family lives of such people — a case of different faces but the same story. Although most of the partners I have worked with have been women, this is by no means an absolute or a given. There are numerous women who exhibit high achievement orientation and have experienced burnout, and their partners have stories to tell that are similar to what is being outlined in this section. Burnout is not exclusive to a particular gender. The partners are invariably supportive and encouraging, but often they find this to become somewhat of a trap where they feel they must continue to offer support, despite seeing unhelpful and sometimes unpleasant changes within their partner.

Life alongside a driven individual can become frustrating and somewhat lonely as they focus increasing amounts of their energy upon the project at hand or future aspects of this. The demands of the task/workplace can see the person working longer hours, often outside of their previous usual pattern. This can bring about alterations to family life and expectations. Partners describe that they need to fit in with the increasing demands of the workplace or organization and that this can lead to a loss of personal identity and their own goal achievement. The latter may also be around what can be done as a couple or a family after the usual working-week hours or on weekends. It becomes hard to plan for outings and events, which, in turn, can lead to the realization that it is often easier to arrange things for and by oneself. Over time, this becomes an easier option and then a familiar one, but at no time have I heard a partner say that this was their *preferred* option.

A challenging time (or crisis point) can arise in the relationship when the supporting partner encounters some difficulties of their own. I have noticed that, in such situations, a number of partners feel they should not 'trouble' the person heading towards burnout. This is because they are often perceived as being busy, focused and under pressure. Unfortunately, this leaves the partner holding back and not expressing or addressing their own issues and needs. Often the partner's personal needs are viewed as something the already busy and stressed person does not need added to their plate. As a result, the partner can be left to continue dealing with the day-to-day issues plus make their own way through the emotional or physical challenges confronting them. At one level, this seems to be viewed as how it has become, while at another level I have had partners describe the situation as 'frustrating', 'unfair' and as though such a situation is devaluing who they are.

ASPECTS FOR THE PERSON WITH BURNOUT TO CONSIDER

All the above can take its toll on the partner. So ... why haven't you, the driven one, noticed? This is the person you are sharing your life with and see each day. I guess it might be hard to realize that there have been things happening that you have not really taken on board. Most of the people with burnout or A/N traits I have worked with continue to have a deep sense of love and caring for their partners. It comes as a shock to hear that their partner might feel as if they have grown apart to some degree. I have noticed that this is not necessarily due to a change in feelings but rather because less time is shared and communication is reduced or changed. Individuals seem to be genuinely shocked to realize that there are new systems and ways of doing things around the home. That these new patterns have developed out of necessity — to fill the gap that came about due to their increasingly lengthy absence — seems also to be quite a surprise.

What's it like for your partner? Well, they often describe a sense of being somewhat trapped. They tend to be proud that their special person (you) is succeeding but also saddened that there is a third party in the relationship: the career or special project. This is a rival that is hard to compete with, given the positives around potential success and advancement. Such an intruder is also complex and intangible, with an unexplained but powerful grasp on the individual. The sadness experienced by the partner doesn't seem to be coming from a place of jealousy. Rather, it is about seeing how their special person is striving so hard and perhaps, over time, enjoying the challenge less and less while seemingly being unable to break away from whatever the demands are. It is also about noticing a subtle change within their person over time, such that priorities no longer represent mutual goals and desires. It can be about altering family scheduling to help avoid the clash between family routines and those after-hours business meetings.

It can be hard for a partner to try to tell you that they are worried (about you), only to be told that everything is 'okay' and under control. It can be frustrating to plan things and then have to cancel them due to a clash with work commitments. It can be upsetting to see the kids yet again not have Mum or Dad come along to the school production. It can be bewildering to realize that they cannot see what is so blindingly obvious: that you are working harder and starting to get run down. It can also be heartbreaking to see the one you love start to doubt themselves and become less confident in areas they previously excelled in and were passionate about.

Manisha was trying to make sense of what had gone wrong in her relationship and where it might be headed. She described being married to a man who was very talented within the IT field. He had apparently been employed by a company that became highly successful on the back of his knowledge, skills and work ethic. However, it took its toll and this man became depressed and extremely anxious, to the point he could not cope with day-to-day tasks, let alone work-based ones.

Manisha stepped up and looked after all aspects of family life while her husband recovered, over a period of months. She described that this was very tiring and emotionally draining, as she also needed to find employment to help with the finances. Interestingly, Manisha did not describe this as the greatest challenge within her relationship. What was most confusing for

Manisha was that once her husband's depression lifted, he immediately formulated plans to start up his own IT company. This saw him operating from home, with no boundaries around the hours he put in; he began rising before 6 a.m. to start the day's productivity and work through till late each night. By all accounts, he worked and lived alongside the family but was so focused on setting up his own company that he had minimal interaction with them. Despite much discussing, arguing and pleading, nothing Manisha said could alter her husband's behaviour. As far as he was concerned, the 'problem' (i.e. the depression) was long gone. Now it was business as usual with potential for greater, self-directed success.

A case of symptoms being addressed but the cause of the problem being ignored, perhaps?

ASPECTS FOR THE PARTNER TO CONSIDER

Life is not a one-way street. In fact, it is more of a tango that we dance with our partners: a complex rhythm that has well-rehearsed patterns to it. The more familiar these steps are, the easier the movement and flow becomes. If you have identified with some of the descriptions above, then perhaps there is a lot going on in your family and relationship. However, this book isn't about apportioning blame. Rather, it is trying to bring about understanding and clarity that may facilitate movement towards a better state of affairs.

So far, we have noted how you, the partner, might have adapted (out of necessity) to maintain the family and its progress. However, this positive adaptation might have also allowed situations to develop that reinforce certain patterns. These, in turn, make it more likely the behaviours of concern will continue (e.g. the scheduling of meetings after hours). If your deft and subtle balancing acts maintain harmony and peace in the family's world, potential problems might be unrecognized by the work-focused or work-committed person. If you view these changes as being unavoidable or you identify with the pressures upon the person, you will be more likely to act in ways that help those behaviours to remain in place. This may have initially been for very sound reasons, of course; for example, you might be very caring, aware of the potential costs to the family unit or perhaps you even share some of those driven traits. The latter can see you over-identifying with what the person is going through. I am suggesting that the social/familial context these behaviours occur in can have a bearing on how well they are tolerated or reinforced.

The key question now is around whether things need to remain this way. There is often little point in simply going on about how and why things got to this particular juncture — that's what this book is doing for you (i.e. helping people make sense of some key contributing variables). Rather, it may now be about what do *you*, the two partners, want to do about this situation. Just worrying about how one ended up at a particular destination is not all that helpful. You might be better off reconnecting and affirming a mutual understanding between you both that things are not as they were and are not as they were intended to be. Ask yourself: is it okay to move towards some change, and might there be some benefits from this for the rapidly burning out individual, for you and for your family? If the answer is yes, then exploring all the variables and behaviours within this book might help you both to see where things went off track and why they have stayed that way. An enhanced understanding may also be one of the keys to opening up the potential for a different future, based on positive change. One that encompasses a better understanding of issues, as well as permitting change without completely overhauling either the relationship or the individual.

TO SUM UP

This way of life takes two to tango. The person heading towards burnout needs someone to deal with life's daily challenges, in order to free them up to focus on the demands of work. The partner is involved by way of filling in the gaps and managing the myriad challenges that come up from the working person not being around. Both people in this dance may be doing things to an extreme, such that an unhelpful system is maintained to the possible detriment of all involved.

The work-focused/committed individual may be distracted from 'real life' due to their narrowed perspective. What they often see around them is a household that runs well and where things get (magically) sorted. This means that the partner's excellent coping is what is on display and this can lead to a false sense of everything running well — there are no problems. If the partner does not share just how much effort is required to maintain this equilibrium it might not be noticed and, therefore, awareness/understanding may have no chance to develop.

Partners have a limit to their tolerance but this isn't necessarily signalled as having been reached until it is too late. They can end up feeling distant, shut out and less connected. They may also find a path of least resistance and establish routines and ways of doing things that don't include the overly busy person!

Now is a good time to see if both of you wish to continue with this dance or perhaps consider whether it is time to change and explore how things might be different for all involved.

A chance for change

The suggestions below are broken up into sections for you (the person with, or heading towards, burnout), your partner, and both of you as a couple.

If you are a driven person reading this book

Your partner is important! They are also the one most directly affected by your behaviours.

Use the information in this book to reflect on how things might have got off track with your family life. Be open to and consider the possibility that there is another (valid) perspective to how things are operating in your life: your partner's. Try to consider what it has been like for them living alongside you, as you have focused most of your energy and efforts on the tasks and roles you considered to be important. If you can see that there may have been some challenges for your partner, perhaps it is time to talk this through together.

If you have been so busy that you have had no time and energy for the 'usual' family things, you might be feeling abandoned by the family as they get on with their lives. You may be feeling overwhelmed or worn out by all the effort you have expended over a long period of time. However, if you cannot clearly express your feelings and accurately describe what you need from your partner, it is hard for them to support you.

Listen to and be genuinely interested in your partner's point of view. Let them express things in their way, not in words you prefer to hear. Acknowledge and validate the feelings and challenges your partner is telling you about.

What if the fear of being judged has become so strong that you can't let your partner know you are actually feeling trapped or are struggling? If you don't try to share what is happening, you might miss the opportunity to gain some support with the challenges you are facing.

If you are the partner reading this book

Central to making and sustaining change will be for the person with burnout to develop an appreciation of how their behaviours affect you, along with an understanding of where this approach to life may have come from. If you are the one who has purchased this book, get your busy partner to start reading (*there is no time like the present!*). Maybe choose a key chapter and get them to read that, before encouraging them to digest the whole book.

Your worn-out partner needs to gain some insight into themselves before they can try to change. Remember, their personality style or workplace expectations have been directing their behaviour for many years. Time to reflect will also be important and necessary — don't place unfair burdens on them to have read a few pages and then have an 'aha' moment. This whole thing might be 'news' to them and, as such, they might have no idea how to begin the change process or know that this is required.

Be open to considering that some of your behaviours could be maintaining aspects of the situation. If your caring nature is such that you prioritize the needs of your partner and feel the need to fix up problems around them, they might feel no need to change. Why would they, when everything seems to get sorted out?

Although this has been a hard journey for you, resist the temptation to demand change and make it happen *now*. It will take time to understand what has been going on and change will be something that needs to be tried on for size. There will undoubtedly be both gains and some slippage with respect to bringing about a change to how one interacts with the world. Don't become despondent if things are not brand new after the first trial at modifying behaviour!

If you are reading this book as a couple

If you can both gain an appreciation of how life has altered, you may be able to work collaboratively to bring about changes that are beneficial for the whole family. Being honest about how you both feel is important, but remember: how you share this honesty is also important. Change is a process. Giving feedback and being open (both parties) to hearing this will enhance the effectiveness of the changes you are trying to implement. You will get better and more durable outcomes if the strategies you implement are agreed upon and seem relevant to both of you.

As has been said in many books and therapeutic situations, communication is the key. Given that the people reading this book may be pressed for time, the focus perhaps should be on the quality of your interactions. You might even need to book a time together in the early stages — this is not colluding with the business approach but simply being practical. However, if there is a mismatch between what you say and what you want to say, opportunities will be lost. It won't be enough to listen to what is being said; you will need to hear it. Remember, even if you have been together for many years, you really cannot read the other person's mind. So don't expect them to do the same for you and know what you really want. Believing that your partner 'should' understand your needs and where you are coming from is simply not fair.

Getting the best out of your efforts to communicate will come from openly sharing how you feel. Of course, how each partner responds is also central to making positive gains. If you can both show some empathy and demonstrate that you have listened to and actually heard what is being said, the channels of communication are more likely to remain open and changes to behaviour sustained. What's that saying about listening with more than your ears?

Here are two tasks you might like to try with your partner. Please note that these are optional.

TRY THIS

Together, come up with six specific challenges or concerns that the current approach to life may be presenting for the two of you and (if relevant) your family. Write them down.

Now, write down — together — three key behaviours or issues from the above that you would like to see change.

Next, I would like each of you to take the perspective of *the other person* and write down *three* thoughts about or responses to the questions below.

For the individual experiencing burnout: What might it be like to be the partner of someone who is so focused on and responsive to work?

For the partner: What might it be like to feel that you must always put everything into the task in front of you and meet the demands of the workplace, despite the costs to yourself?

CONCLUSION

Life can be ironic at times. You spend years developing abilities and gaining experience and then use these to help you achieve to high levels. You continue to work hard, gain respect and tick off the goals you set. Yet you end up feeling distant from these gains, being unsure of where you're at and struggling to find the enthusiasm that once was ever present. Doesn't seem fair at all, does it? I get that there was no deliberate plan to end up where you are currently headed or have recently been — wrestling with the effects of burnout. Unfortunately, though, this is what you've encountered and have been trying to deal with.

The aim of this book has been to help you understand that burnout is something that can increase to a point where it affects your health and wellbeing plus impact all aspects of your life. By understanding what might be both contributing to and maintaining its presence, you will be in a better place to manage the negative effects. I would encourage you to relate to this book as you would the act of looking into a mirror. It's a way of reflecting back to you how you are presenting yourself. It can give you some feedback and insight into what is happening for you, and a chance to make some adjustments based on what you now see in front of you.

Recall for a moment what it was like looking in the mirror first thing this morning. You might not have liked what you initially saw and perhaps thought you were not looking your best. However, there was an opportunity to adjust and make your presentation different/better, so that you could head into your day (or life) in a confident manner. This confidence comes from the adjustments that you made, following the awareness that you developed from looking in the mirror. In the same way, this book can be that opportunity to see yourself in a light or manner that has been reflected to you, and now you have the chance to make changes to important aspects of yourself.

There are some consistencies showing up worldwide regarding who is vulnerable to burnout and, indeed, who might be leading the charge towards it. Prime amongst these is the overachiever, the committed and very conscientious employee or executive. While the company may love you and your approach, this other-oriented perspective will, most probably, have been costing you personally. The fact that you cannot give anything but 100 per cent effort, 100 per cent of the time, means that you are setting yourself up to develop burnout. Cue the irony again: if you love what you do and you are good at it, you are also going to be really good at justifying (to yourself) why you are doing it in the manner that you are!

After getting to this stage of the book, you will hopefully have a better understanding of burnout and how it has affected your world. I would now like to encourage you to be bold and make some choices about how you want your life to look going forward. Surely, there is room for more joy, spontaneity and a greater sense of fulfilment? This may well mean that there are increasing layers of good stuff in your life, enhanced vibrancy related to what you do, and simply a more pleasurable journey through the next stages of your life.

My work as a psychologist involves promoting and facilitating behaviour change. It is something that I feel strongly about, as it can open up new directions in life and bring about greater satisfaction. I do not accept the old adage that 'you can't teach an old dog new tricks'. I can change, and you can change. However, it's not a passive process. The key to shifting from where you have been is to be active, make deliberate choices, and use the skills that you have been reading about in this book. Simply stopping, taking a break or going on vacation isn't going to alter the impact of your burnout. You will most likely just return to doing the same things, in the same way, for the same unknown reasons as soon as you return to the workplace. Additionally, you will have just wasted your precious vacation time as you were probably too exhausted to enjoy it! Better to start working on the things that are going to fill your tank up again. See that refuelling as encompassing anything and everything that is important to you as a person — your physical, emotional, behavioural and spiritual dimensions. This can be your time to shift your priorities to what you need. Take the opportunity, via the knowledge you have just gained, to understand where you are at with your mental wellbeing and put in place options that can support you and build you up. It's important to start making positive efforts around your wellbeing. Otherwise, your body and brain are going to require you to address your 'unwellbeing'.

TRY THIS

Right now, make a commitment to do the following:
- Take your permitted breaks during the workday.
- Ensure that lunchtime is just that — a time to be away from your workstation (actually eating your lunch) in a space that is not demanding that you attend to work-related tasks.

- Schedule your vacation for a time that works for you and your needs. Saving it for 'later' is costly, in more ways than one.

The past is a place of reference, not a place of residence.
— Roy T. Bennett

Although it often hurts to think that you didn't do so well in the past, it is possible to learn from what you have been through. You don't need to be stuck with overwhelming feelings of regret and anguish. Once you realize that certain behaviours and ways of relating to life have unhelpfully dominated and directed your life, you can look to make a change going forward. Experience can be a fearful and haunting presence, or it can be a good teacher. You can move forward and pick a path that better suits you and who you want to be. This is my hope for you, as you read and reflect upon all that is within this book.

The information and skills have been presented as a way of making sense of what you are heading towards or have been struggling with (the experience of burnout). They give you the basis to make sense of things. However, that is not the end point. You will benefit further from honestly reflecting on how the information relates to you, your approach to work and/or the responsibilities of your life. The next step is doing something about this. This is where the skills and suggested options come into play. They build the bridge from the knowing to the doing. Without the latter, you will be stuck with increased insight but no change, and that is a recipe for frustration. So, I strongly encourage you to look at when and how you can take the management options presented to you and place them into your daily life. This will allow you to begin the change process and refine it, based on what you find works for you.

Burnout does not need to be a life sentence. Even though you may have limited opportunities to change your work environment, you can make positive changes to those aspects of yourself that you take to work every day. As mentioned earlier in the book, your strengths may well have become your vulnerabilities and resulted in you becoming susceptible to the effects of burnout. However, you do not need to throw away your sense of discipline or your desire to do well in life. The 'new' you can continue to use your key attributes but in a more managed and directed manner. Think of a dimmer switch on your lighting system at home. This lets you choose the best amount of light for a given situation. The same can be achieved with your abilities and personality style. By adjusting how much you let those schemas and historical tendencies come to the fore, you can apply them in a way that helps you to achieve but not set you on a path of 'too much, too often and too hard'.

In Chapter 5, I talked about 'turning the tide'. Now that you can understand the pressures and drives within yourself, you can make a shift towards a place where you call the shots and choose how to apply your strengths, but now in conjunction with and guided by your wider aims and values in life. It is not too late to change the script that you have been operating by and alter the trajectory of your life in a manner that is more sustainable and provides a more meaningful way of working and living. Going forward, I would like to encourage you to trust your 'new' self, and look forward to a life that is more balanced and follows goals that you have consciously chosen to reflect your more complete self.

BIBLIOGRAPHY

Agassi, A., 2009, *Open: An autobiography*, Three Rivers Press, New York.

Bamber, M. & McMahon, R., 2008, 'Danger: Early maladaptive schemas at work! The role of early maladaptive schemas in career choice and the development of occupational stress in health workers', *Clinical Psychology and Psychotherapy*, 15, pp. 96–112.

Covey, S., 2004, *The 7 Habits of Highly Effective People*, Simon & Schuster, New York.

Ellam-Dyson, V. & Palmer, S., 2010, 'Rational coaching with perfectionistic leaders to overcome avoidance of leadership responsibilities', *The Coaching Psychologist*, vol. 6, no. 2, pp.81–7.

Frankl, V., 2008. *Man's Search for Meaning*, Ebury Publishing, London.

Garcia, H. & Miralles, F., 2016, *Ikigai: The Japanese secret to a long and happy life*, Hutchinson, London.

Hayes, S.C., Luoma, J.B., Bond, F.W., Masuda, A. & Lillis, J., 2006, 'Acceptance and Commitment Therapy: Model, processes and outcomes', *Behaviour Research and Therapy*, 44, pp. 1-25.

McCracken, L.M. & Velleman, S.C., 2010, 'Psychological flexibility in adults with chronic pain: A study of acceptance, mindfulness and values-based action in primary care', *Pain*, 148, pp. 141–7.

Mogi, K., 2018, *The Little Book of Ikigai. Live a happy and long life the Japanese way*, Quercus Editions Ltd, London.

INDEX

A

acceptance 37, 53, 60, 70, 97, 157–59, 167, 181, 182, 194, 196, 197; *see also* accommodation
acceptance and commitment therapy (ACT) 69–71, 112, 147–48, 151–52, 176
accommodation 69, 71, 90, 157–58, 167, 172; *see also* acceptance
achievement 54, 106, 120, 180–81, 182
   achievement-focused life 124–25
   high achievement 40, 87, 88, 89, 91, 92, 115–16, 121, 153–54, 202
   personal achievement 35, 40–41, 86
   in the workplace 2, 8, 11, 12, 13, 14, 23, 26, 52, 82, 89
adaptability 146–47, 148, 172–73, 181, 183, 189–90, 191, 194, 196–97
affirmation
   within the family 33–35, 38, 40–41, 48
   see also reinforcers; rewards
Agassi, Andre 35–36
airline pilots 45–47
all or nothing (A/N) personality 25–27, 39, 47, 112, 145, 147, 155
   health behaviour and care 120, 121, 123, 128, 129–30, 141
   partner of a person with A/N personality 200–06
   perfectionism 36, 54, 106
   self-criticism 82, 85, 91
   see also driven personality
anxiety 14, 68, 84, 86, 111–12, 116, 133–36, 137, 142, 143, 157
appraisal 20, 45, 47, 57, 58, 79, 85, 95, 157, 176
automatic behaviour 24, 32, 70, 148, 149, 150, 152, 158, 176
   and internal criticism 56, 85, 92, 97, 98, 118
   see also schemas

B

behaviour 3, 11–12, 13, 19, 32, 57, 136; *see also* schemas
behaviour change 65–66, 214–17
'black and white' thinking 93, 108
boundaries 15, 23–24, 81, 140, 206
breaks 7, 66, 68, 122, 215
breathing techniques 5–6, 70, 141, 143
burnout
   description and causes 1, 2, 3, 6–9
   World Health Organization definition 2–3
business professions 17–19

C

career choice 44, 48, 52, 181
caring for family members 15–16
caring professions 14–15, 48–49
change: exercise to look at doing things differently 42–43
'choice point' concept 67–68
circle of influence 74–75, 78
cognitive behavioural therapy (CBT) 112, 133, 143
commitment 13, 14, 26, 141, 176, 180–81, 207, 208, 214; *see also* acceptance and commitment therapy (ACT)
competitiveness 13, 14, 32–33, 89, 125
completion *see* task completion
confidence 2, 9, 36, 56, 58, 77, 84, 85, 95, 116, 136, 144, 175, 179, 190, 196, 214
conscientiousness 51–52, 79, 101, 214
control 22, 41, 55, 59, 62, 64, 102, 127, 137, 165, 177, 179, 180, 191
   control by parents 33–36
   enhancing control 71–79
   letting go of things 75–76
   Stephen Covey's model of control 73–75
counsellors 14–16, 143

criticism 36, 38, 40; *see also* internal critic
culture of the company 7, 125

D

deadlines *see* timeframes and deadlines
delegation of tasks 80, 107, 114
depression 14, 111, 130–33, 142, 143, 157, 205–06
diaphragmatic breathing (belly breathing) 5, 143
disengaging 92–94; *see also* engaging with work
dissatisfaction 2, 6, 181
distancing 6, 16, 27, 148
doctors
  consultation by people with burnout 121, 124, 125–26, 127–28, 130, 132, 142–43
  susceptibility to burnout 14–15
driven personality 54, 91, 101, 120, 121, 126, 129–30, 141, 147–48, 153–54, 158
  origins of a driven personality 30, 32, 33, 35, 38–39, 40–41, 42
  partner of a person with a driven personality 200–06
  response to schemas 45, 47, 48, 124
  self-criticism 85, 87, 89, 98
  see also all or nothing (A/N) personality

E

ego-dystonic 18
embarrassment 86, 87–89, 91, 93, 95
emotionally-driven behaviour 70, 75, 157–59, 189, 198
emotions 1, 3, 6, 15, 28, 68, 83, 88, 90, 92–93, 95, 173, 189, 191, 192–93, 194, 198
empathy 15, 212
energy 1, 3, 4, 9, 18, 54, 64, 68, 72, 74, 86, 117, 136, 137, 190, 192–93, 201, 209
engaging with work 29, 32; *see also* disengaging
expectations of performance 4, 7–8, 13, 17, 18, 19, 33, 68, 94, 107–08, 116, 125, 148
  family expectations 31, 33–36, 37–38, 39–41, 44, 49
  peak performance 56, 116, 142
  personal expectations 20, 26, 39, 46–47, 56, 111, 116–17

F

failure 26, 36–37
  fear of failure 37, 41, 50, 56, 59, 87, 90, 115, 120, 136
  potential failure 37, 54, 56, 87, 89, 135, 136
family 25, 27, 102, 109, 121–22, 154
  family of origin 30–32, 39–42, 48, 122
  see also home life
fatigue and exhaustion 1, 6, 9, 15, 16, 27, 129, 215
feedback on performance 12, 22, 96, 211
  negative feedback 85–86
  by parents 32, 33–35
  positive feedback 86, 108
fight or flight response 134–35
flexibility 147–52, 157–59, 160–63, 166, 168, 170, 172–73, 189, 191
  tips for kickstarting flexible thinking 150–51
friendships 27, 130, 154, 179, 182, 186, 201

G

generalization 32, 136
goals 50, 52, 106, 142, 170, 217
  consistent with values 30, 144
  goals *versus* values 153–54
  personal goals 2, 12, 68, 105, 176, 177–78
  self-generated goals 25, 26, 27, 116–17, 118
  unmet goals 119, 136
  in the workplace 2, 8, 11, 88, 125

H

happiness 142, 181
health 25, 121–22, 141–42
  effect of previously learned attitudes 122–25
  making changes 142–45
  minimizing problems 126–30
  see also psychological health
home life 14, 25, 102, 136; *see also* family
hours of work 7–8, 13, 15, 18, 49, 88, 147

I

ikigai 180–83; *see also* purpose
internal critic 36, 38, 41, 46, 55, 56, 82, 94–95, 157, 197

Index **221**

approaches to change 96–97
impact of self-criticism 86–89, 109, 132
and perfectionism 105, 106–07, 110, 114–16, 117–18
stepping back from negative internal comments 89–94
techniques for dealing with internal criticism 98–100
understanding self-criticism 83–86
see also negative feelings and thoughts

J
journalling 140–41
judgments from others 12, 23, 36, 50, 86, 116, 210; see also self-judgment

L
leadership 12, 17
legal profession 13–14

M
meaning 180, 183–86
  exercise 184–86
meditation 18, 141, 143
mindfulness 69–70, 139, 141, 143, 182
modelling of behaviours 11–12, 13, 31, 36, 42
mood problems 111–12, 116, 130–33, 196
motivation 2, 25, 28, 131, 143–44, 180

N
negative feelings and thoughts 54, 55, 56, 64, 65, 68–71, 76–78, 83–85, 192, 197; see also internal critic
nurses 14–15

O
occupations susceptible to burnout 10, 12–19
optimism 182, 190
options 47, 70–71, 99, 176, 177–79, 190, 191
  health behaviour and care options 123–24, 126, 131, 132–33, 138–39, 143
  perspectives on options 146, 147, 148, 149–50, 167–68, 170
  response to schemas 50, 58
outcomes 2, 26, 28, 50–51, 56, 105, 120, 124, 136
consistent with values 31, 32, 34, 40, 144
risk of focusing on outcomes alone 2, 106, 109, 120–21

P
parents 44, 49, 122, 152
  control 33–36
  critical comments 38, 40
  feedback from a driven parent 32
  as role models 31, 36, 40
  understanding parents' behaviour 41–42
partner of a person with burnout 200–03, 208–09, 211–12
  aspects for the partner to consider 206–08, 210–11, 212
  aspects for the person with burnout to consider 204–06, 209–10, 212
  tasks for partners to try together 212
peer group culture 32–33
perfectionism 14, 16, 22–23, 30, 35–36, 45, 50, 54, 55, 56, 58, 79, 80, 101–03, 115–17
  approaches to dealing with perfectionism 110–15, 117–19
  defining perfectionism 105–06
  problems 106–10, 111–12
performance punishment 23
personal characteristics and burnout 10, 12, 19–24
personal identity 55, 64, 87, 203
personality style 14, 51–53, 105, 121, 129–30
perspective 32 34, 57, 58, 79, 93, 96, 105, 146, 149–50, 155–56, 159–61, 163–68, 170, 189, 190, 194
  perspective-taking strategy 171–72
predictability 38, 59, 60, 73, 149, 151, 196
prioritization 20–22, 24, 25, 26, 33, 50, 68, 125, 141, 149, 215
problem-solving 45, 69, 75, 97, 137, 138, 143, 168, 183, 190, 192, 194, 197
procrastination 37, 101, 119, 136
psychological health 14, 123, 130–41, 143; see also anxiety; depression; mood problems; worry
psychologists 14–15, 103–05, 143
purpose 175–79, 183–86; see also ikigai

222   *Beating Burnout*

R
recreation 25, 32, 154
reflection exercises 28, 29
reinforcers 2, 8, 11, 25, 28, 32, 44, 115, 144
   within the family 31, 35, 38, 40, 42
   see also affirmation; rewards
relationships 27-28, 52; *see also* friendships
relaxation 68, 141, 143
resilience 181, 188-90, 198-99
   attributes of a resilient person 193-94, 195-96
   benefits of being resilient 191-93
   ways to enhance resilience 196-98
responsibility 16, 18, 26, 50, 56, 79-81
rewards 31, 34-35; *see also* affirmation; reinforcers

S
schemas 19, 44-49, 53, 57, 58, 79, 113-14, 118, 123, 124, 126-27, 169, 188, 217
   examples 50-51
school 121-22
self
   sense of self 41, 58-59, 89, 120, 144, 159-60, 168-69, 181, 194
   separating thoughts and ideas from self 163-66
self-doubts 46, 56, 57, 65
self-efficacy 73, 75, 78, 115, 139, 193
self-image 55, 160-61
self-judgment 70, 84, 91, 93, 106, 109, 117
self-reflection 63-64
'self-sacrifice' schema 49
shame 87-89, 109, 132
sleep 18, 68, 202
slowing down and changing 155-56
SMART goals 153-54
social workers 14-15
spontaneity 59-60, 151, 214
standards
   expectations of other people 107, 113-14
   setting standards 105-06, 111, 112, 113, 116-17, 119
   standards aligned with rigid thinking 108-09

stress 2, 6, 131, 142, 143, 198, 201
   minimizing stress 75-76, 77, 141, 142, 143, 182
   workplace stress 3, 4, 6, 11, 14, 22, 48, 80, 110-11, 116, 129, 145
success 32, 36-37, 39, 50, 52

T
task completion 25, 26, 48, 50, 103
   family values 30-32, 35, 37, 40
   feelings and thoughts exercise 61
timeframes and deadlines 7, 13, 17, 20-21, 37, 55, 68, 81, 125, 136, 158-59
tiredness *see* fatigue and exhaustion
tolerating negative thoughts and feelings 68-71
triage model 21-22

U
uncertainty 22, 65, 76, 79-80, 136, 137, 138, 179, 181, 191, 194, 197
   intolerance of uncertainty 54-57, 58-60
underperformance 39, 82, 87, 89, 101
urgency *see* timeframes and deadlines

V
values 2, 8, 142, 144, 145, 151-52, 155-56, 169, 178, 179, 184-86, 194
   goals *versus* values 153-54
   identifying your values 154
   values exercise 169-70

W
'wait and see' attitude 59
wellbeing 2, 11, 14, 26-27, 39, 75, 121, 124, 128, 136, 142, 144, 192, 213, 215
work ethic 14, 35, 36, 50, 205
work/life balance 14, 17, 25-26, 27, 67, 68, 145, 149, 151, 170
workload 4, 7, 13, 20, 23-24, 79, 80-81, 107, 145
workplace 1, 4, 7, 121-22
   inadequate resources 4, 7, 15, 72
   the main cause of burnout 3, 6-7
World Health Organization definition of burnout 2-3
worry 7, 59, 62, 69, 70, 134, 136-38, 143, 158, 180, 181, 191, 193, 199
   worry awareness exercise 138-41